Sharlot Hall on the Arizona Strip

Sharlot Hall
on the Arizona Strip

A *Diary of a Journey Through*
Northern Arizona in 1911

by Sharlot M. Hall

Edited by C. Gregory Crampton

NORTHLAND PRESS

Library of Congress Cataloging in Publication Data

Hall, Sharlot Mabridth, 1870–1943.
    Sharlot Hall on the Arizona Strip.

    Bibliography: p. 95

    1. Arizona—Description and travels.   2. Hall,
Sharlot Mabridth, 1870–1943.   I.   Title.
F811.H17   917.91′04′40924   74–76087
ISBN 0–87358–127–X

FIRST PRINTING

ISBN 0–87358–127–X

Library of Congress Catalog Card Number 74–76087

Composed and Printed in the United States of America

Contents

Preface

ANY RESEARCH on the life and times of Sharlot Hall must begin in the Sharlot Hall Museum of Arizona, Prescott, where Miss Hall's personal papers and her extensive collections on Arizona history are on file. Additional primary materials will be found in the holdings of the Arizona Department of Library and Archives, Phoenix; the McClintock Collection, Arizona Room, Phoenix Public Library; Arizona Collection and Special Collections, University Library, Arizona State University, Tempe; Arizona Historical Society, Tucson; Southwest Museum, Los Angeles.

In the pleasant task of editing Sharlot Hall's work on the Arizona Strip, I have studied in all of these institutions, and some others, and I am much indebted to numbers of dedicated staff members for their assistance. For special advice and help I thank Lester W. Ruffner of Prescott and Michael Harrison of Fair Oaks, California.

Sharlot M. Hall's work reproduced here with some variation bears the title "Diary of a Journey through Northern Arizona and the Arizona Strip." This is a revision of the original title, and I have divided the chapters differently than those of the original and added chapter headings. Sharlot Hall's formal narrative ended with Chapter X. From an abbreviated diary she carried along on the trip and from a newspaper account she wrote later, I have pieced together an itinerary that forms the contents of Chapter XI. Beyond this, editorial intrusion has been minimal. Hall uses *vermillion* for the cliffs rather than *vermilion*. *Pah Ute* for the Indian tribe is now usually spelled *Paiute,* and *Pahreah* (the river and plateau) is now *Paria. Moen Copie* for the stream is now usually written *moenkopi.*

Rather than resort to footnotes I have added a short introduction to each chapter for the purpose of clarification and perspective. In a brief introductory essay, I have tried to show that Sharlot M. Hall left her mark. Indeed, she was one of Arizona's most interesting and influential pioneers.

C. GREGORY CRAMPTON

Introduction

SHARLOT MABRIDTH HALL was one of those rare women of her day—a literate child of the American frontier. As soon as she could talk she began making up songs and verses and in one of the early grades, while supposedly laboring at geography, she wrote out her first book of verse on the yellow pages of "The Farmer's and Mechanic's Note Book," issued by a patent medicine company. This "first edition" showed her early interest in history for it contained verses on Columbus, the Spanish discovery of Florida, and ballads about Indian fights and frontier life. And at about age fifteen she broke into print with some poems composed on the hurricane deck of a horse.

Sharlot Hall stayed with poetry throughout her adult literary life. She made verses easily, the best of them springing from her own experiences and the rough-and-tumble life of the frontier. Her reputation as a writer seems to rest on two books of collected poems: *Cactus and Pine, Songs of the Southwest,* issued in 1911, revised and enlarged in 1924; and *Poems of a Ranch Woman,* published posthumously in 1953 by the Sharlot Hall Historical Society, Prescott, Arizona. Both titles are kept in print by the society. In a biographical sketch published just before her death in 1943, Charles Franklin Parker referred to Sharlot Hall as "Arizona's beloved *poetess laureate.*"

This title tended to obscure the significant fact that Sharlot Hall had written prose as well: travel articles, short stories, essays. She was fond of the essay. In her lengthy bibliography one may find articles on politics, cooperative marketing, photography, hired men, and on being single. She was an enemy of injustice, intolerance and cant. One title, "Americanism, a Sermon," was more than a sermon; it was a blast (it "came up like a volcano in my mind") against the hypocrisy and emptiness of post World

War I "red-blooded Americanism." Another piece, "Why Women Want to Leave the Farm," was an essay on the dreary slavery endured by so many farmers' wives on the frontier. But her strongest prose genre was history—of Arizona and the Southwest. She produced no books but her collected historical pieces would fill a volume or two, possibly more.

Sharlot Hall was caught up in the American westward movement; she was a part of it, she loved it all and was one of its better interpreters. Much of her writing, poetry and history, she said once, was done to make others "love and understand" the westering American. Indeed, her works belong on the same shelf with those of Elizabeth Custer, Martha Summerhays and Carrie Strahorn, all of whom she admired and publicly extolled.

Sharlot Mabridth Hall was born on October 27, 1870, the first white child in Lincoln County, Kansas; when she was nine the family moved to Barbour County near Indian Territory. She later recalled that she was born, brought up and educated among Indians and that in those thinly-settled districts the women were few. "The people of my baby days," she said once, "were all men—hunters, trappers, soldiers." Just after Sharlot's eleventh birthday, the family moved once more, this time to Arizona. The young girl rode all the way on horseback. Remembering the ride she wrote years later: "In mid-February of 1882 I rode into Prescott on a long-legged, dapple gray mare who had just left her foot-prints on the full length of the Santa Fe trail. We had been three months coming—three winter months with covered wagons and a caravan of loose horses [which she herded along]—like Abraham and his family seeking new grazing grounds."

On Lynx Creek, some twelve miles southeast of Prescott, the Halls settled at a place they later called Orchard Ranch. Since her father was a partial cripple, Sharlot through her teen-age years helped out on the ranch branding cattle, milking cows, splitting wood, picking fruit, and even panning gold when the family went into placer mining for a few years. The young girl did finish the grades at a small country school four miles from the ranch and boarded out in Prescott to attend one, and her only, term in high school. Since the Halls had scarcely prospered, Sharlot felt compelled to return to the ranch where increasingly she assumed the burden of management as her parents' health declined.

But Sharlot Hall refused to be ground under by the hardships of pioneering. Prompted and encouraged by a mother she adored, the young ranch woman took a lively interest in Arizona, its Indians and prehistoric peoples, its frontiersmen and early pioneers, many of whom she met on trips to Prescott, the territorial capital of Arizona until 1889. Through the years she

2

found time to publish a few poems and magazine articles but her literary career was not fairly launched until she came to the attention of Charles F. Lummis of Los Angeles, colorful, crusading editor of *Land of Sunshine,* a monthly regional and literary magazine devoted primarily to southern California.

Sharlot Hall read the magazine and when an article on camels on the deserts of the Colorado appeared in it, she sent in a very short piece giving supplementary information on the history of camels in Arizona. Lummis ran it in the issue of February, 1898, and encouraged her to send in more contributions. She responded with poems and articles. Lummis was so impressed that in 1901 he invited her to join his staff. Introducing her in his regular column "In Western Letters," in the issue of April, 1901, he wrote that Sharlot M. Hall was "a genuine young frontierswoman—not of the cheap drama and Sunday-edition counterfeits, but a fine, quiet, loveable woman made strong and wise and sweet by life in the unbuilded spaces." Of her writing Lummis said it was "always vital, lucid" and imbued with an "unmistakable thrill of humanity." Her work was informed but "never academic." Her poetry "always means something—as so much magazine verse does not."

Sharlot Hall went up fast. Soon after she joined the Lummis organization the editor decided to enlarge the scope of *Land of Sunshine* and to change the name to *Out West.* For the first page of the first issue Lummis wanted a poem to celebrate the name change. He asked both Edwin Markham and Joaquin Miller for something suitable but neither responded. He then told his new staff member that she would have to furnish the poem. The result was Sharlot Hall's "Out West," issued first as a broadside and mailed to every magazine of note in the United States, and then published in the first number of *Out West,* January, 1902.

Lummis was delighted with the poem. "The noble stanzas which open this number (page one) are of a rare sort," he editorialized in the January issue. A ranch woman from Arizona had written a "greater poem" than other poets of the time seemed capable of. The work was widely copied, praised by professors, set to music and collected in anthologies. The author included it (under the title, "The West") in her own *Cactus and Pine.* In a prefatory note she tells us that the poem was written out during part of one day—November 25, 1901. The theme of the work appears in the last line: "That man among men was the strongest who stood with his feet on the earth." The poem has point today, for men still "grow small in the huddled crowd, / And weak for the breath of spaces where a soul may speak aloud."

Shortly after this triumph Miss Hall's name was added to the long list of prominent writers and artists who made up the "staff" of the magazine. Among her associates were such southwestern lights as Maynard Dixon, Frederick Webb Hodge and Washington Matthews. Later Sharlot Hall appears to have shared with Lummis some of the editorial duties of the magazine but she seems not to have been tied down to any regular assignment. She commuted frequently between Los Angeles and Arizona where she gathered material for articles and kept in close touch with her parents at the Orchard Ranch.

During her years with *Out West* Sharlot Hall contributed over forty pieces, articles and poems in about equal number. Most of her work was inspired by the environment, people, times, and history of Arizona. Titles on Prescott, Tombstone, camels, stock raising appear in the list of historical items, and there are long pieces on Indians, forests, reclamation, deserts, and health-seeking.

Out West for February, 1906, was a notable number. Almost all of it was written by Sharlot M. Hall. First it contained one of her best known poems —"Arizona" (reprinted in *Cactus and Pine*), a work written in response to a move by Congress to admit to the union as a single state both the territories of Arizona and New Mexico. The proposal was hotly opposed in Arizona. When Sharlot learned that President Roosevelt had endorsed the plan, she rushed home to the ranch and, again, in but the part of one day, dashed off a scornful, sarcastic work calculated to shame the perfidious eastern lawmakers who would "sit at ease and grudge us our fair won star." Sharlot Hall said later that the territorial officials had the poem printed in broadside and placed on the desk of every member of Congress. It was read from the floor of both houses and reprinted widely.

The February issue of *Out West* also carried a sixty-eight page study of Arizona's economy designed to show that the territory was a land of bountiful resources being developed by God-fearing men living at peace with one another in busy thriving towns and communities. The article was written, the editor added, to correct the "amazing misconceptions popularly current," that Arizona was peopled by train robbers, desperados, gamblers and prostitutes, such "grotesque misinformation" having been "purveyed by the common, or garden, variety of short-story writer."

The publication of these works in *Out West* assured them a fairly wide audience since the magazine in 1906 enjoyed a circulation of about ten thousand copies. The author made no claim for the effectiveness of her works in the cause for which they were written, but Congress in 1906 did

4

amend the joint statehood bill permitting the two territories to vote sep-
arately on the question. Arizona resoundingly rejected the proposal and
Congress went ahead to endorse separate statehood which both Arizona
and New Mexico achieved in 1912.

After serving *Out West* for nearly a decade, Sharlot Hall resigned in 1909
to accept a position as Territorial Historian of Arizona. For her contributions and her achievements as a woman, she was much appreciated at
home. When the legislature created the office of historian her candidacy
was advanced by the Woman's Clubs of Arizona. For some years the clubs
had fostered the study of history and ethnology and they were convinced
their candidate was the best in the field. So was Republican Richard E.
Sloan of Prescott, the last territorial governor, who made the appointment.
The governor, no doubt, looked into Sharlot's political views before he
named her to the post. She always thought of herself as a Republican but
she "took her politics gently," voting as she saw fit in elections. Actually the
first incumbent, a man and a Democrat, was replaced after he had served
only a few months. Sharlot Hall took office on October 1, 1909, the first
woman in Arizona's history to serve in public office.

The historian by law was expectd "to faithfully and diligently collect
data of the events which mark the progress of Arizona from its earliest day
to the present time, to the end that an accurate record may be preserved of
these thrilling and heroic occurrences" and "to publish the same in book
form when completed." The salary was good for those times: $2400 per
year and $1800 travelling expenses.

Moving into her office in the State Capitol at Phoenix, Sharlot Hall began
investigating the extent of collections of books and documents in Arizona in
private hands and public institutions. But her primary interest was to preserve the reminiscences of the living witnesses of Arizona's history. The
books and documents will be available long after the last pioneer has been
"called to cross the Last Frontier," she wrote.

And so, in order to collect oral history, to become familiar personally
with historic places, which would enable her to write intelligently of all
parts of Arizona, Sharlot Hall from July, 1910, spent well over a year in the
field. Remote districts were reached by making long trips with team and on
horseback. By her own words she "visited every city and nearly every town
and mining camp in Arizona," and every county but Santa Cruz. In July,
1911, the "longest wagon trip" was begun, the purpose being to visit the
Arizona Strip, "that little known region lying north of the Colorado River."
Sharlot Hall's report of that journey forms the body of this work.

Some of the finest plateau and canyon landscape anywhere is found on the Arizona Strip. Save for the Virgin Mountains astride the Nevada boundary on the west, The Strip consists of five parallel, elongated plateaus of sedimentary rock separated by long lines of colored cliffs, or steep slopes, running from the Grand Canyon north to the Utah boundary and beyond. The general ruggedness of the region is enhanced by deep, sharp-rimmed canyons, and by a vast volcanic field in the western part.

The Powell Survey had made geological studies in the Strip country in the years from 1869 to 1880, but those who came to know it best were the members of the Church of Jesus Christ of Latter-day Saints. Moving southward from Great Salt Lake, the Mormons planted the first white settlements along the middle reaches of the Virgin River, in Utah, where the climate was temperate and the water plentiful. From St. George, in the heart of Utah's "Dixie," The Strip was open and inviting and throughout the region by 1870 the Mormon interest had become altogether predominant. Once it gained statehood in 1896, Utah took a lively interest in The Strip and several bills were introduced in Congress calling for the annexation of the region north of the Grand Canyon. Arizona objected to these moves, but The Strip was cut off from the rest of the territory by the 279-mile length of the Grand Canyon. "Very few of our people know anything about it," Sharlot wrote.

On her extended trip into The Strip country, Sharlot Hall had two goals in mind. One, she wanted to complete her historical tour of the territory, and two, she wanted to learn as much as possible about "that great corner of Arizona" in order to inform her fellow citizens about the area Utah was hoping to annex. Her publications had helped prevent the merger of Arizona and New Mexico. Her findings on The Strip, if given to the public, might help thwart the designs of an aggressive neighbor. Accordingly, she made arrangements with John Arden Reaves, publisher of *Arizona, the New State Magazine*, a promotional monthly, to run a series of articles in the form of a diary of her journey.

Sharlot herself found it difficult to get very much information ahead of time about roads, water, or the general lay of the country north and west of the Grand Canyon. The advice given by a sheriff and a stockman was: "Don't go." But she was determined to have that "stray history, no matter how hard it might be to round up, so I hired a guide at Flagstaff and with his stout travelling wagon and a pony team that could stand the rough roads, I started out" July 23, 1911. The guide was Allen Doyle. "We carried grain for the horses for a month, a water barrel to tide us over the desert stretches which we were told might be long, and the lightest camp outfit that it seemed possible to get on with."

For the next seventy-five days the two people traveled leisurely along, camping wherever the time and place seemed right. They struck north from Flagstaff to the Little Colorado where they picked up the road to Lee's Ferry opened by the Mormons in the 1870's. Indeed, wherever they went on The Strip, they followed the roads and tracks opened by Mormon pioneers. From the ferry the travelers went through House Rock Valley and across the Kaibab Plateau. Twelve glorious days were spent on the Kaibab and on the North Rim of the Grand Canyon, which Sharlot wrote about in some detail.

Pushing on westward the travelers visited Kanab, Pipe Spring, Hurricane, Zion Canyon and the Mormon villages along the Virgin River. From St. George it was a long, rough haul to the Grand Gulch mines. After that they edged into Nevada, crossed the Colorado River into Arizona and headed south, visiting mining districts in the Cerbat Mountains. Finally, on October 3, 1911, the weary travelers reached Kingman, on the main line of the Santa Fe. After roughing it so long, what a welcome sight, Kingman and the railroad! Sharlot described her feelings: "From a hilltop we saw the dark smoke of a puffing railroad engine and I did indeed say some prayers of gladness—for a thousand miles in a camp wagon is no joke, even when every day is filled with interest and the quest of fresh historical game."

Sharlot Hall's *Diary* in eleven installments ran intermittently in *Arizona, the New State Magazine* from October, 1911, to April, 1913. For six months after September, 1912, no installments at all appeared. When they were resumed the editor explained that Sharlot Hall's mother had died and the author herself had fallen ill. The diary in published form was never completed; it broke off halfway through the trip. However, from Sharlot's very abbreviated *Diary,* which she carried along, and from a summary account she wrote for a newspaper dated January 29, 1912, I have been able to work out the itinerary and put together an account of the travelers' experiences for the remainder of their remarkable trip.

Sharlot Hall's "Diary of a Journey" is one of the earliest works descriptive of the Arizona Strip at large, its people, resources and history. She did not cover the entire region but she visited nearly all those places where development of some kind had occurred. Furthermore, this was the only one of her travels as territorial historian that was reported in print. Sharlot Hall's articles certainly drew attention to The Strip country. In 1914 the

State of Arizona sent an official party, scientists—A. M. McOmie, C. C. Jacobs, and O. C. Bartlett—to make a brief survey of the agricultural possibilities and water resources of the area. Their official report underlined and emphasized much of what Sharlot Hall had published in her "Diary of a Journey" but they dwelt on farming and little else. Territorial Arizona, one supposes, was a man's country, but it took a woman to put some of its most rugged country on the map.

Sharlot Hall's work on the Arizona Strip has gone unnoticed by the historians and even by those who have written biographical sketches of its author. It does not appear in the bibliographies. Files of *Arizona, the New State Magazine* are scarce. It is time to re-introduce to the public "Diary of a Journey," one of Sharlot Hall's most important prose works.

The "Diary" climaxed the most productive part of Sharlot Hall's literary career. When Arizona was admitted to the union in February, 1912, she resigned as territorial historian and apparently did not apply for the position of state historian and librarian created soon thereafter by the state legislature. This decision also meant giving up the preparation of a projected three-volume history of Arizona. Her mother's death in August, 1912, and her own illness—a recurring malady of the spine brought on as a result of a severe fall from her horse on the trek to Arizona, 1881–1882—seem to have sapped her spirit. After a serious spinal operation she retired to Orchard Ranch but wrote very little for the next ten years.

But she was not forgotten. In 1921 the University of Arizona awarded her an honorary bachelor of arts degree. Then in 1922 a small group of Prescott business and professional men, who called themselves the Smoki, and who were developing a yearly pageant based on Indian themes, asked Sharlot to write a booklet describing their purposes and objectives. She obliged with *The Story of the Smoki People,* a work which rekindled once again her interest in writing. In 1924, she brought out a second edition of *Cactus and Pine,* first issued in 1911 just prior to the death of her mother to whom it was dedicated. Both these works were well received and brought their author back before an admiring public. She was asked to run as one of Arizona's Republican presidential electors in the national election of 1924. By the other electors she was chosen to hand-carry the state's vote to Washington and she stayed on to witness the inauguration of Calvin Coolidge.

In the second edition of *Cactus and Pine* Sharlot Hall expressed hope that the book might open the way for the publication of "many of those wonderful human documents I have found" written by Arizona's pioneers. The dream was not realized. Sharlot herself did not feel impelled to publish. From time to time she was urged to write up her experiences of frontier life. She was intrigued and even supplied the title: *Essays of a Ranch Woman*. But the essays were never written. "It has never seemed to me to be a matter of importance whether my own writing was published or not," she wrote in the 1924 preface of *Cactus and Pine*.

When her father died in 1928, Sharlot Hall moved to Prescott where new interests took up most of her remaining fifteen years. The Sharlot Hall Museum in Prescott is a monument to the work she accomplished during these years. She restored the "Old Governor's Mansion," a large log building which had been the territory's first capitol and the home of its early governors. It had been acquired by the state in 1917 with the expectation that it would become a museum, but precious little had been done before Sharlot Hall leased the building. She moved into it and donated her own extensive collections of artifacts and relics, papers and documents; she solicited and gathered additional materials reminiscent of Arizona's pioneer times. Another log building—"Old Fort Misery"—was moved to the grounds. In the 1930's she secured federal emergency relief funding to construct a fine large stone building which now houses some of the museum exhibits, the library and research center, and the offices of administration, including those of the Sharlot Hall Historical Society.

Sharlot Hall died on April 9, 1943, at the age of seventy-three. She never married but when she was "half past fifty" she wrote out part of an essay entitled "Being the Happiest Woman I Know." Her love of Arizona, everywhere evident in her works and writings, was only exceeded by her love of life. As Sharlot wrote in one of her favorite poems, "Cash In": "O life is a game of poker, and I've played it straight to the end." Someone asked her once if she were a feminist. "No," she replied, "I'm a humanist, not a feminist." On the opening leaf of the diary she carried along on the 1911 journey to the Arizona Strip, this appears in her own hand: "There is something better than making a living—making a life." She clearly chose to live. After reading many of her poems, essays, historical pieces, letters and fragments, I can say with conviction: "She made it."

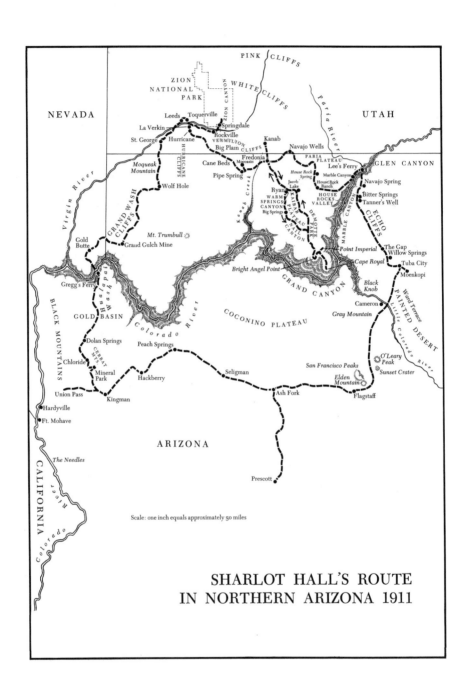

**SHARLOT HALL'S ROUTE
IN NORTHERN ARIZONA 1911**

The Diary

Arizona's Unknown Treasure Land

Sharlot Hall was the first booster of the Arizona Strip. During a leisurely journey of observation, lasting nearly two months, she crossed its deserts and plateaus and made notes about nearly everything as she went. This chapter is a summary of what she learned about a region then, and now, virtually unknown in its entirety to Arizonans and the rest of the world.

⊷ THE COLORADO RIVER, entering Arizona from the north, bends southwestward in a big elbow, several hundred miles long and walled the whole distance with the most wonderful cliffs in the world—as if some huge mountain chain had been torn apart to make a channel for this most kingly river west of the Mississippi.

The same great walls that shut the river away from the world make a wild and all but impassable barrier between the region lying north of and within the elbow and the country to the southward—the mainland, one may say, of Arizona.

Even on the northern side the country is fenced in with long, rough mountain ranges, and canyons woven back and forth like a mighty net; with sand washes where great rivers could lose themselves among vast sweeps of polished black boulders, and dune-trailed mesas where today's roads are blotted out by the night's wind whipping up sand banks around the "old man sage" and the saber-leaved yuccas.

Nature, herself, built the walls around this treasure vault and it is not strange that she has kept her secrets so well.

I cannot give the acreage within this elbow without reference to compiled data, but it includes about one-third of Mohave County and a good-sized section of Coconino, enough to make some of the Atlantic states and have pieces left over.

There are several roads leading into this region from the south side of the Colorado River, none of them good, and none so bad as to be impassable for a good team and strong wagon. Any one of them will emphasize the need for a wagon bridge somewhere on the Colorado River for at the present time crossing must be made by ferry boat, which in high water is very dangerous.

Perhaps the best wagon route is the old Mormon road from Kanab to Lee's Ferry and thence by way of the Painted Desert and Tuba City to the Little Colorado River and from there to Flagstaff, and southward.

No road in Arizona passes through wilder, stranger, or more grandly beautiful scenery, and with the state road completed to Flagstaff it is no distant dream that the highway may be extended northward and a region absolutely unique opened to automobile travel, creating an avenue for trade with a part of our own state that now goes to Utah for all its supplies.

Arizona has the largest unbroken forest in the world and the least-known part of it lies on the great Kaibab Plateau, or, as it is also called, the Buckskin Mountains, directly north of that part of the Grand Canyon in the vicinity of Bright Angel camp. Here, almost unknown to Arizonans, is a forest containing over three billion feet of merchantable lumber, fine yellow pine, spruce and fir, "ripe," as lumbermen say, for cutting. The spruce alone would furnish a large supply of paper pulp but one can wish that it may not soon be used, for these spruce forests, reaching like a great green cloak over the softly rounded mountain tops and along the open parks, are beautiful beyond telling.

This whole plateau will one day be a playground for the nation—a playground unique in its grandeur and offering attractions not to be found anywhere else in the world.

The United States government has already recognized this and has made of a part of the Kaibab Plateau the largest national game preserve in the world. This preserve already contains about eight thousand deer, according to the estimate of the game warden, and as no shooting is allowed at any season on the preserve the number is increasing. In the fall the deer drift down into the foothills and may be shot during the open season.

It is known that elk once roamed over this forest region and a movement is on foot to bring in this fall a portion of the herd being moved out of Wyoming. Game experts say the region is ideal for elk, offering shelter of the sort they like best and their favorite food, the tall bracken fern.

Few know that in this forest and the House Rock Valley below it may be seen a herd of buffalo roaming as they did over the great plains. At present they are privately owned, but every effort should be made to induce the government to buy this herd and to furnish the means for systematic breeding. The commercial possibilities will be seen when it is known that a good animal is worth about $2000. A good robe sells for a thousand dollars and often more, and a good head for five hundred dollars.

The buffalo thrive on this range and buffalo farming might be developed in northern Arizona as ostrich farming has in southern Arizona. It is certainly a no more fantastic idea than was the taming and commercial development of the ostrich on farms.

There is also a fine herd of the rare Persian sheep on the Kaibab, valued at about $400 each, and giving excellent promise of becoming a large factor in the sheep industry of the future. These are the large-tailed sheep that furnish the finest mutton known, and from the unborn lambs comes the Persian lamb fur, which at its perfection, commands fabulous prices.

The growing of ordinary grades of sheep and cattle is the oldest industry of this region. The range has been stocked since the early eighties and the principal assessable property is in livestock. Most of this is owned by citizens of Utah and is moved about as range conditions vary, so that there is considerable difference in the tax roll from one year to another.

While the range has sometimes been overstocked, as have all the cattle ranges of Arizona at one time or another, there is possible a good deal of increase in the business, especially in Mohave County, through the development of water and the consequent opening up of unused ranges.

From the pine forests, where in years of normal snow and rainfall the grass is fine, the range descends through cedar-covered foothills and rolling mesas to the wide valleys that are only about three thousand feet above sea level and warm accordingly. This has been a great sheep country; and the wild range horses have increased till they have become a nuisance in some places, and steps are being taken looking toward the public disposal of them, as was necessary a few years ago in some parts of Nevada.

The mines of the Grand Canyon region have always been a lure to the prospectors and unusual finds have been confidently predicted. The most interesting realization of this expectation has come during the present year, when it has been proven that the gold-bearing clays and deposits from the San Juan into the Colorado River contain free quick-silver as well as flour gold. These curious banks, as richly colored as an oil painting, extend for one hundred and fifty miles up and down the river, and across into the Painted Desert.

At present they are being worked by the Lee's Ferry Gold Company, with headquarters at the famous old John D. Lee ranch. They have two gasoline boats and a steamboat on the river and expect to develop the coal fields near the river for use on their property.

Gold has been found in the bars along the Colorado River since the sixties and has been mined in a small way, but the distance from points of supply has forbidden large development. The new bridge on the Little Colorado River to be built this winter will do much to develop the mines of all the region beyond, and will doubtless lead to new discoveries. This river, with its bed of ever-shifting quicksand, has claimed, old teamsters say, enough wagons to make up an army wagon train and has discouraged travel into the Painted Desert and Big Colorado region.

Better roads through this region would open up vast deposits of gypsum and probably of borax and various sodas, for many of the clay hills are crusted with crystals and snow-like deposits.

This, too, is the region of petrified wood, which extends northward into Utah, and of many and varied agate beds where stones of much beauty and some value may be picked up on the surface of the ground. These range from beautiful banded agates and those showing the curious oxeyes to solid-colored stones in a wide range of colors.

Throughout the whole region of the Colorado River sandstones in wonerful brilliancy of colors and beauty of grain and markings abound and could be quarried for building purposes. There are limestone regions, too, of wide extent, and ledges of gray blue stone of beautiful texture, not unlike a fine oil stone.

The sandstone cliffs of all this region carry some mineral values, silver, gold and copper, and there is a good chance that valuable mines will be found in places where no prospecting has yet been done. The Silver Reef, one of the great silver mines, lies in these cliffs and the richest copper mine in Arizona is surrounded by cliffs and ledges and terraced buttes of rich red sandstone as vivid and beautiful as the Vermillion Cliff or the wine red sandstones at Lee's Ferry.

This mine, the Grand Gulch Copper mine, has been worked for forty years and has never shipped ore running less than thirty per cent copper. Car load lots have gone better than forty-five percent and the choicest ore has assayed eighty per cent. There are now hundreds of tons of ore on the dumps, ranging from thirty per cent downward to seven and waiting good roads to make it available.

All this region was better known to prospectors thirty years ago than it is today, and farther southward toward the "Big Bend" of the Colorado

River, fortunes were taken out in placer gold as well as in silver and copper. The coming of the Santa Fe railroad and the end of steamboating on the higher reaches of the river pulled the prospectors southward—old roads and trails fell into disuse and for years the land has been all but deserted, because of the expense of getting in and out.

However, it is neither in mining nor stock-raising that the greatest development of much of this beyond-the-canyon region will be found. In all parts, between the mountain ranges and the great cliffs that cut in and out across the country, are valleys of great extent and of rich, deep soil—such valleys as, in the adjoining part of Utah, are producing under scientific dry farming better crops than are produced by the irrigated areas of the same state.

The greatest valleys of southern Arizona are hardly more extensive and are no better situated for large home regions. Probably sufficient water for irrigating much of this land can be and will be developed—already immense irrigation projects have been mapped out and are seeking capital. The people of Utah are as wide awake to the value of this "Arizona Strip" as the people of Arizona have been asleep to it since the territory began. With the advent of statehood and some means of buying state lands many settlers who have already selected the land they wish to own will make haste to cross the border, and within another quarter of a century this unknown part of Arizona will rival the richest of the central valleys in population and products.

But if it is to be Arizonan in spirit and truth and if the turn of the tide of wealth as it develops is to flow toward Arizona, wagon roads must be pushed northward, streams must be bridged, and railroads must be encouraged under wisest conditions.

Already this region has "paid its way"; the tax rolls of Mohave County show for the past two years, respectively, $7,426.33 and $6,123.03, of paid-up taxes coming from its northern third, which on the other hand has cost the county very little during that time.

Of the scenic beauty of this region it is impossible to say enough; the northern rim of the Grand Canyon is incomparably grander than its southern mate and it is cloaked to the very brink by as noble a forest as can be found in the Southwest. The highest point rises 9000 feet and from it one can look across the mighty chasm and over two hundred miles of Painted Desert beyond.

Farther west in the Mt. Trumbull region is a volcanic area as extensive as and even wilder than that northeast of Flagstaff. Here, too, is another forest belt where forty years ago a saw mill was brought in by the Mormon settlers of southern Utah and lumber cut for the great temple at St. George, and for the settlements along the Virgin River. A small mill is still in operation at Parashant on the Arizona side.

Geologically, one of the wonders of the world is the great Hurricane "fault," reaching southwestward from the Pink Cliffs of Utah into Arizona, a huge slide in the earth's crust that has left a vast plateau walled with massive cliffs some hundreds of miles long and sheltering in its mighty trend valleys where the climate is warm enough that figs, peaches, apricots and grapes come to a perfection which even California cannot better. It is, indeed, more like Sicily with its vineyards, rooted in volcanic ash, and as the Utah part—"Utah's Dixie Land"—is already famous for its fruit, so the Arizona end of the "fault" will some day be celebrated.

All over this region are prehistoric remains of past settlements, and the later Pah-Utes and Navajos have contended sharply for the country in the first days of its present settlement. At the present time there are probably not two thousand white settlers.

TWO

Down to the Little Colorado

Reading up for the trip ahead Sharlot Hall found Frederick S. Dellenbaugh's Romance of the Colorado River *(1904) an excellent reference. The author had traveled with John Wesley Powell's second trip down the Colorado, 1871–1872, and he had participated with Powell in a systematic survey of the lands north from the Grand Canyon to the base of the High Plateaus in Utah. These activities, briefly summarized by Dellenbaugh in his* Romance, *were more fully elaborated in his* A Canyon Voyage *published in 1908, a work which Sharlot Hall apparently did not see.*

For her companion and guide Hall engaged one Allen Doyle, an Arizona pioneer of 1872. Doyle had gone into mining and stock-raising around Prescott, where Sharlot met him. He moved to Flagstaff in 1885 and began guiding tourists to the Grand Canyon and other points. We learn from a newspaper account published in 1896 that he was a man of "discretion, good judgement and genial disposition." Doyle is mentioned by name in Sharlot's diary of the trip but not in the published account where he appears only as "my guide."

Their light Studebaker wagon loaded and the two Arabian ponies harnessed, the travelers left Flagstaff July 23, 1911, and headed north toward Tuba City and Lee's Ferry on a dirt road closely paralleling today's U.S. Highway 89. Between the summer showers they enjoyed beautiful vistas of the San Francisco Peaks, Sunset Crater, O'Leary Peak, and of the cinder cones and lava flows found all about on this great volcanic field of which the San Francisco Peaks is the center.

Dropping down through the pine and juniper forests they came out into the open grass country where the Painted Desert, "filled with strange masses of color," came into view off to the north and east. In the west the thousand-foot high mass of Gray Mountain dominated the landscape.

Camp for the second night was made on the Little Colorado River swollen by the muddy runoff from summer rains. Nearby was the spot where in 1897 Fleming Parker, aliases Jim and William Parker, was taken into custody by George Ruffner, sheriff of Yavapai County. Wanted for train robbery and murder, Parker was sentenced and hanged at Prescott, Arizona, in June, 1898.

ᡃᓍ FOR SOME MONTHS I had been planning to cross the Colorado River at whatever point might seem best and to travel over that part of Arizona which lies north and west of the river and the Grand Canyon. There is hardly another region in the West that is so little known to the outside world, and certainly no other part of Arizona has been so little considered by the rest of the State.

The engineers of the Geological Survey have been over the section and Frederick Dellenbaugh, who accompanied Major Powell on his last trip through the Grand Canyon, has written of the country in his *Romance of the Colorado;* but nonetheless, the whole area included in the "Arizona Strip" is so little known south of the Colorado River that it was impossible to get any definite information as to the best way of reaching it.

My purpose being to gather all the historical data possible, as well as to inform myself about the country and conditions, I decided to follow the wagon road known as the "Old Mormon Road," which crosses the river at Lee's Ferry and continues northward into Utah, and over which many Mormon settlers came into Arizona and Mexico in early days.

From the very meager information I could gather, I knew that I must expect very rough roads, for there is little travel through the whole region and heavy summer rains cut and destroy the roads year by year. On this account I wished to take a strong but light traveling wagon and horses sufficiently light and active to be good mountain climbers.

I knew that there would be places where water must be carried for the team, though how far and over what kind of roads I could not learn. It was certain, too, that much of the way would be without grass and that as much grain as possible must be taken along. In addition I did not expect to be able to buy food after leaving the last Indian trading post beyond the Little Colorado River, and I was obliged to consider carrying food enough for two people for a month or six weeks.

This meant consideration of every pound that went into the wagon; space as well as weight counted, for it is no joke to get all the things that two people and a team will need for a month or two into one covered spring wagon. It meant leaving behind everything one could possibly spare—then looking at the wagon and leaving half the rest.

Sacks of horse feed and boxes of canned goods built in carefully around the water barrel made the bulk of the load; there was no room for camp chairs or folding cots, or more than a regular prospector's cooking kit, and the only thing granted space without question was the camera and its supplies. It took several days at Flagstaff to plan and pack and make sure that none of the necessities were left behind and few of the extras taken.

I had been able to engage for the trip a man whom I had known for years and who knew the road for the first three days out, and who was himself a pioneer of 1872 and not likely to find many new experiences on the journey. From the time that we left the Indian school at Tuba we would be on roads unknown to us and must be guided by such information as we could get as we went forward. This meant no particular anxiety to us, for we were both accustomed to "roughing it" and to getting over wild country. I shall let the diary of the trip tell the rest of the story.

JULY 23. We got away this morning about ten o'clock, after trips to the drug store, grocery, post office, and various other places to gather up the "last thing" needed for the trip. I had no idea when I should get mail again, so I could not bear to go on till I knew if the morning train would bring a letter from my mother, who had not been well. No letter came and I am obliged to go on, uncertain, but hoping everything will be right.

A week of heavy rain around the San Francisco Mountain has made the roads very muddy and little pools stand all along the low places, but the forest is glorious. The road led out along the base of Elden Mountain, and on either side the fields of oats and barley were green and fresh. These farms have nearly all been started within the past three years and make a remarkable change in the landscape; every little park and bit of open valley between the forest spaces has its well-fenced fields, and some very good houses have been built so lately that the yellow of the new lumber stood out against the green pines like a splash of sunshine.

The land here is rich and for years the finest potatoes grown in Arizona came from the little parks in the Mogollon Mountains; but it seemed odd to find thrifty, promising grain fields and permanent homes where cattle and sheep and deer ranged when I first saw the country. Much new land has been taken up this year, for there were new fences and fields just broken up out some fifteen miles.

All beside the road the lavender pink "spider plant," the *cleome pungens* [*serrulata*], had grown up into tall thickets, and I saw hovering over it flocks of what I thought to be butterflies, but as we came near they proved to be hummingbirds, little brown fellows with red spots on their heads and green-backed ones as bright as the eye on a peacock feather. The airy, feathery blossoms were like a great pink cloud and the tiny birds darting swarms above seemed like animated jewels; I could scarcely believe they were real birds.

White plumes of vapor and drifting rain clouds were hovering over the San Francisco Peaks and patches of snow showed in many places; the peaks have a sense of grandeur, of over-towering greatness, from this eastern and northern side, which is most impressive. Elden Mountain was just too low to touch the floating clouds and the sun falling full over it made the curious great ribbed ledges which form its top, stand out as if carved with some mighty knife.

Geologists say this mountain is unlike any other in Arizona; from top to bottom it is ribbed with great, wide sweeps of rock that look like the side of a bulged-up cone of gray-yellow-brown mud, just hard enough to crack into squares and patterns and crumpled ridges, but not hard enough to be safe to walk on. There are smooth, shining patches that look like a permanent temptation to go sliding, and down-sweeping canyons, awesome and dusky in their deep plunges.

The pines cling green and dark wherever they can find footing, but much of the wild, beautiful mass of rock is bare and looks, somehow, like a kingly human head bared in reverence of the vast and noble beauty around it. A famous geologist who was out with my guide a year or two ago, said it had been formed by volcanic action pushing up a huge portion of earth-crust, still only half cooled and hardened.

We stopped to water the horses at the Greenlaw saw mill, just around the foot of the mountain to the east; a new mill which is already reaching out toward Sunset Mountain [Crater] and the Cinder Beds with its little logging railroad. We followed the road along through the narrow, park-like valley toward Sunset and the way it went rambling off after every patch of fine timber and crawled up against the cinder patches reminded me of an old cow pony who is going to follow his bronco steer if it climbs a tree. In fact, the logging railroads of this part of Arizona do everything except climb a tree—and they get the trees they start after if they have to swim a lake or jump a canyon to do it—as some of them have done.

Out beyond the sawmill we took the Tuba road through a long park that ran like a green river between the deep banks of pines. The grass was tall enough to mow and all among it great patches of rose-colored loco blossoms stood up above their silver green mats of leafage, so vivid and rich and clean from the summer rains that the color ran back into the forest like streaks of wet paint.

My guide said that on one of his trips with a surveying party an Englishman in the outfit gathered all he could carry of the loco and came into camp with it and told the boss that he "Found a bloomin' fine feed of red clover for the horses, don't you know." He was mightily disappointed to find the harvest of his kindness hustled out of camp and to be told what the new kind of "red clover" would do to the stock. This part of the mountain must be a bad horse range, for we found many patches of the white-flowered loco as well as of the rose.

Prairie dogs have taken up their own sort of homesteads on this side of the mountain in the past few years and barked at us from little towns and scattered holes all along, even in the shady forest, which is not the home they usually choose. The gray squirrels have increased since shooting them was forbidden two or three years ago, and now and again one would chase across the road with his fluffy tail curled over his back, and dart up the trunk of a pine, scaring some black and white spotted woodpecker into fits and making him drop the worm he had been boring out of the bark.

The rain clouds gathered thicker on the San Franciscos, but on the right hand and before us the wonderful lava region was spread like a picture, dappled over with cloud shadows and spots of gleaming sunshine that brought out everything like the lens of a reading glass. The big, flat-topped cone of O'Leary's Peak was in front, and beside us on the right, with the exquisite green basin of Bonita Park between, Sunset Crater stood draped in its wonderful colors.

Earlier in the day a heavy shower had fallen and the great mass of cinders and lava which makes up the crater beds out of which it rises, and which here extend for miles through the forest in long, narrow strips and smoothly-rounded "whale-back" dunes, rippled and streaked like sand dunes on a windy coast.

The dunes and the base of the cone were an intense blue-black, deep and yet bright; and the rain-soaked sulphur crust and lava of the upper two-thirds had deepened and ripened into softest rust-browns and brown-reds and mellowed sulphur tones, till under the dappling sunlight it looked like nothing so much as a huge late Crawford peach. The very velvet bloom was there, so soft and tender and half-mysterious that one would not have

23

been surprised to see the whole mountain melt away into some shadowy, sun-painted cloud.

While I was trying to photograph the tiger-skin lights and shadows, the rain swept down off the 'Friscos and the park and cones were lost in walls of falling water. Only Black Crater, set in between O'Leary and Sunset, stood in a rift of light like a big bowl set out to catch a family supply of rain water.

This Black Crater is one of the most perfect cinder cones in the whole volcanic region and its deep inner bowl is as perfectly shaped and rounded as if scooped out by hand. Some tall pines in the bottom look like quite ordinary trees from the rim. There is a place on the side of this crater from which one can speak in an ordinary tone of voice and be heard distinctly more than a mile away across the cinder beds.

With the rain beating against the wagon curtains, which we had put down and fastened in a hurry, we drove through the pine forest and out into the lower, cedar-covered foothills, our road following in a curve north and east around the base of the great peaks. No one who has seen the San Franciscos only from the Flagstaff side can have any fair idea of their grandeur; they grow in size and sense of huge bulk mile by mile, as one goes out on this Tuba road.

From the foothills over which we were driving the great plateau base on which the peaks stand is uplifted like the pedestal of some gigantic monument, and soon the peaks detached themselves one by one from the great mass into which distance had blended them until seven distinct and grandly carved heads stood out, four lower, three towering into the very center of the clouded sky; and in a sudden flare of sunlight the far, sharp point of Mt. Agassiz rose up as if standing erect to look over the heads of his brothers, so that eight true peaks were lined against the clearing sky.

The rock-clefts and deep-scarred canyons at the top were lined with drifts of snow, and below this barren foothold of winter the forest swept down from the gnarled and vine-like creeping spruce and fir of upper timberline to the thick, green cover of magnificent yellow pine, broken with patches of pale green quaking aspen and with one big gray scar of a forest fire.

The cedared foothills blend into a high, irregular valley which has been a fine stock range, but which will some day, and probably in a very few years, be covered with grain fields and homes. There is hardly a more beautiful location in Arizona, and the soil is good, good enough at least to grow as thick a crop of grass as one would wish to see. There is no permanent water on the surface except a few little springs in the foothill canyons, but there seems no reason why water should not be gotten by sinking wells.

I wanted to photograph the San Franciscos from this side, and as it had been too rainy and dark all afternoon we made camp in the cedars on the top of a rolling range of foothills, where the morning view would be fine. We had driven till late and it took so much time to make camp and get the load sort of untangled that I did not trouble to have my little tent set up, but hunted out a thick-branched cedar tree and spread my blankets under it, trusting to chance that it wouldn't rain before morning. There was plenty of dry cedar for the campfire and I wrote by the light till too sleepy to see.

JULY 24. Long before daylight I had my head out from under my "tarp" bed cover to watch the stars fade and the sunrise come. The whole eastern sky was full of feathery bits of cloud that turned from faint pink to red and finally to gold that fairly glowed. The big peaks were perfectly free of cloud or fog and as the sun rose they turned to the most wonderful blue; every canyon and ridge of cliff as clear and sharp as if broken out of blue glass.

From the knoll, half a mile from camp, where I went to get my pictures, the valley dipped down in a gentle slope and then up again till it ran into the forest at the foot of the peaks and was lost. It was probably from five to ten miles across, dotted and broken with cedars, and the wet grass glistened in the sun till the whole thing looked like a narrow sea channel filled with little islands.

I now saw O'Leary's Peak and Sunset Crater from the eastern [she means western] side (they shut in the southern trend of the high valley), and they, too, were more beautiful than I had seen before. The chain of crater cones begins again at the northern end of the valley and swings in a curve eastward toward the Little Colorado River. Some of them are most perfect in shape and of very curious formation, one large cone looking exactly as if molded from strips of taffy candy.

This part of the lava region is seldom visited because water must be carried a long way and there is no road that goes very near, but it is wilder and finer than the country better known. The cinders from a few inches to many feet deep look as if blown out of a railroad engine yesterday, and vary from tiny grains to good sized lumps, blue-black or gray or a dull, long-burned red—harder to walk in than a sand bank and dragging wearily on the horses.

We met some people yesterday who had gone out on this road a few days before and found the Little Colorado so high that they were afraid to cross, so turned back to Flagstaff. This may mean an indefinite delay for us somewhere on the river bank and there is no grass there. We have been able to carry only hay enough for a few days, so may be obliged to drive up the river to Black Falls and try to cross there where the bottom is rock instead of quicksand.

From the top of the cedar ridge, as we drove out from camp, the Painted Desert came into view so suddenly and was so dim and cloud-like, blending into the clouds that had been so bright at sunrise, that I mistook it all for a cloud. I could not take my eyes away from it as we drove on; the whole eastern horizon was filled with strange masses of color, reds and blues and yellows and gray-browns, cut and carved into the most fantastic shapes and swathed in mysterious smoke-like haze that blotted out all sense of solid earth and rock and sand.

At our feet another park-like valley rolled away, full of good home lands in spite of having the gruesome name of "Dead Man's Flat" hitched to part of it. Some poor fellow tried to make his way across it years ago and was found dead near the road—a stranger hastily buried in an unmarked grave, with somewhere someone waiting sad-hearted for his return.

In a little canyon beside the road we found a tiny spring called Indian Seep, and near it a good-sized circular shelter of freshly-cut cedar boughs. We were glad enough to find this camp; we knew that somewhere ahead was a freighting outfit of ox teams on their way to Lee's Ferry, with machinery for a mining company, and we hoped to make the crossing of the river with them instead of alone, and to get information from them about the Ferry road.

The country ahead is bare of grass and wood; yesterday we cut all the kindling we could carry from a pitch pine log and filled all the space under the wagon seat and even in front where our feet are supposed to go. It is no fun starting a fire of wet weeds and soggy greasewood and sage (which don't burn half as well as the name would lead you to think), and I expect this "fat-pine" to come in handy. We are leaving the cedars behind so fast that we stopped at the last dead one and put on as much dry cedar as we could tie to the side of the wagon with the halter ropes.

Heavy showers began almost as soon as we had gathered our firewood. They make the red, sandy earth so bright that every little stone showed up, and I walked as much as I could to hunt agates. This is the queerset country, lava and cinders follow down from the mountains in long streaks, but the canyons running into the Little Colorado are walled with dark red sandstone that looks burned to a cinder and lies in big, cracked-up blocks like broken bread-crust.

In several places there was a capping of lava flow that seemed fresh enough to be hot and still moving, and the whole region is a tangle of sandstone cliffs and ridges burned and eroded into the most fantastic shapes by wind and blowing sand. There is no more weird and ghostly country in the whole Painted Desert. Lower toward the river the whole upper strata seems to be eroded away and piles of curious pebbles, smooth as if polished, are scattered all about. In places they looked just like a fall of fresh hailstones, and we named one place the Hailstone Hills.

We were trotting along in the rain and little spurts of hail when we rounded a bunch of hills and came on the outfit of the Lee's Ferry Mining Company camped for dinner. They had eight or ten big wagons and a long string of Texas cattle, reinforced with a lot of wild steers bought at Flagstaff the week before and just getting broken to the yoke.

The Texas "bulls" were big, wide-horned dun and clay-bank fellows who had "been there before"—for they lay right down in the road as soon as the wagons stopped and were chewing their cuds as calm as a lot of cows in a milk yard, the yokes tipped this way and that to ease the pressure on their necks. Most of the broncos in all stages of limping soreness were rounded into a herd and humped up with their backs to the hail, while a couple of herders rode around them.

The "bull-whackers," most of them as green at the business as the bronco steers, were hunting shelter under the wagons and waiting the dinner call. The wagons were big, old-time freighters coupled out to accommodate all sorts of stuff, and on one a thirty-horsepower gasoline launch was navigating the desert preparatory to pulling barges up the Big Colorado River to the mines.

The boss of the outfit told us they would pull into the Little Colorado that night and camp near us, so we hurried on. As we dropped down to the river the country looked like it had just come out of the oven; the canyons and washes leading toward the river are all rimmed and walled with dull brown sandstone that looks like clinkers from a burned brick pile or broken crusts of over-baked bread. It is eroded into weird and fantastic shapes, all sere and cinder-looking; ruins of cities and walls so real that I can understand how easily the prehistoric pueblo-builders hid their little homes among them. Several times we thought we saw Indians off from the road, but it always proved to be just some sliver of the sandstone standing up out of the ledges.

There is little soil in this section, the black volcanic cinders run down in strips and the rest of the mesas that drop down like steps are red and yellow sand and great washes of pebbles ground and polished by ages of rolling in some lost ocean. I picked up agates of many kinds, banded red and white and black, and white and moss agates of good quailty.

We pulled into the river in a sandstorm; across in the Painted Desert the water from the shower just done was running down in a big sheet of silver to the river, but around us every grain of sand seemed caught in a small cyclone and bent on cutting away the whole face of Tish-la-pai Mountain. All day this huge remnant of some lost plateau which the Navajos call "The Gray One" (Tish-la-pai), has shut us in to the north [actually to the west].

It has the curious likeness to a big, blunt-nosed shark stretched out, steely gray above the sandstone canyons; the sides wrinkled with deep-cut water marks, and Mesa Butte making a knobby tail back toward the upper line of the San Franciscos.

We made camp on the bank of the Little Colorado where Parker, the train robber and murderer of Lee Norris, was turned over to Sheriffs Ruffner and Cameron some years ago by Preston and the Navajos who captured him out in the desert. It took some coaxing to get my little pointed "squaw tent" to stay up, even when it was anchored to a cottonwood limb, and more coaxing to get fire enough to bake bread for supper.

THREE

Tuba City and Moenkopi

The Little Colorado was never predictable in the summer when the rains came. At times the stream might be a mere trickle, at others a roaring flood thick enough with mud to make good adobe, as the bull-whacker said. The ford located at the head of the canyon of the Little Colorado was known as Tanner Crossing. Before the year 1911 was ended a steel bridge was put across the canyon one mile downstream at Cameron, thus eliminating the hazardous ford and opening the northern country to increased travel.

With the help of the mining outfit Sharlot Hall and Al Doyle forded the stream without trouble and headed across the Painted Desert toward Tuba City. Sharlot was enthralled by the rounded, brilliantly colored, hummocky hills of the desert bounded on the west by the brooding Black Butte, now called Black Knob, or Shadow Mountain, and on the east by the intricately eroded facade of Ward Terrace. Reaching Moenkopi (as this word is usually spelled today) Wash our travelers found it flooding and they made camp not far from the ashes of artist Frank P. Sauerwein. Maryland born, Sauerwein had moved west and lived much of his life in Denver. Since Fred Harvey was one of his patrons he painted scenes along the Santa Fe Railway and apparently was captivated by the marvelous colors of the Painted Desert.

After much difficulty in crossing Moenkopi Wash, the travelers finally arrived at Tuba City oasis. Attracted by fine springs in the vicinity, pioneering Mormons, headed by Lot Smith, settled here in the 1870's; their properties were acquired by the federal government in 1903 and converted to an administrative center for the huge Navajo reservation. Streets shaded by Lombardy poplars and bordered by green grass were most welcome to desert travelers in Sharlot Hall's day and since.

On July 29, Sharlot visited the Hopi (Moqui is the older word no longer used) town of Moenkopi, a rather prosperous offshoot of Oraibi village some fifty miles to the east. Moenkopi was founded by Chief Tuba in the 1870's on ground that had been occupied by Hopis earlier, and before them by prehistoric peoples who abandoned the place about 1300.

≈§ JULY 25. The river roared all night like a regular surf; a fresh "rise" came down after dark. The banks here are low sand flats rimmed with cliffs of the red-brown clinker-like sandstone, and in the biggest floods the water probably goes from wall to wall. The bull-whackers say you could "cut good 'dobies right off the top," but there is no grass and we must cross or go somewhere else.

The men crossed the teams at noon; hitched a couple of spans of horses in front of a long string of yoked cattle and drove them over and back to settle the bottom. They say the river has swallowed enough wagons at this crossing to make an old-time army wagon train.

The wagons came jolting down the steep bank and into the river with a splash, and rocked and rolled in the sand and muddy water. The cattle were up to the middle in the deepest channel but did not have to swim. The bull-whackers had left all their extra clothing on the bank and they splashed along beside the teams, yelling and popping the big whips and using language that had been accumulating compound interest since the first "bull train" crossed the plains.

They got over all right, wagon at a time, but at every little stop the wheels began to sink as the river bottom sucked hungrily. Two of the men on horseback tied ropes to the end of our wagon tongue and rode ahead, pulling from their saddle horns to keep us moving. The water splashed the wagon bed and I held the camera on my lap. The Navajo mail carrier came along from Tuba City, riding with his feet pulled up on the pony's back in mid-channel; he said the Moen Copie (now usually spelled Moenkopi) Wash was bank-full and fords all gone.

The bull teams went into camp as soon as they got across to shoe up a lot of the wild steers. They were a sorry lot of foot-sore, yoke-bruised cattle and some of them had fought so hard against being made part of a trans-portation system that they came close to being pounded steak on the hoof. Ordinarily a wooden frame is used to swing up the oxen so they can have the two-piece iron shoe nailed on, but this was not possible on the road, so they were roped and "hog-tied" and shod with no ceremony and remarks that seemed close to welding heat.

Leaving the river, we struck northeast across the desert through a chain of low, perfectly rounded clay hills in the most vivid colors, red streaked with white, slate-blue, and a green so clear that in the distance I thought we were coming to green grass for the horses. The hills are small, often grouped together over a clay flat, and look so like cocks of hay in a field that I called them the Haycock Hills.

They seem to be the fragments of some earth-layer almost eroded away; in many places they are crusted with some sort of salts like frost crystals and after a good wetting in a shower the surface "rises" just like biscuit dough when the baking powder is put in. It works into cracks and puffed blisters and in walking over it one crunches through this crust.

The mining company whose outfit we left at the river is working similar clay on the Big Colorado for flour placer gold. They say all this desert carries, in this particular formation, gold values from fifty cents to five dollars the cubic yard. Much of it is unknown except to the Navajo Indians and it seems likely that future prospecting will discover various mineral substances of value, if not the precious metals. Black sand is to be seen in every little wash and the iron stone of placer districts.

All afternoon we bore to the northeast and the country grew wilder and more unlike any every day earth; above us to the east the rim of a great plateau broke off in cliffs of clay and sandstone from fifteen hundred to two thousand feet high and gorgeous and fantastic, with a fringe of stunted cedars dark as India ink along the top. There was little vegetation of any sort; now and then a clump of green brush.

Near us the hills were topped with toad stools and caps and gnome-heads of harder clay, standing on slender necks that would fall in during some rain and strew the ground with still more strange blocks, and the polished pebbles which filled certain strata like plums in a cake. The ground was shining in spots with the paint-like mud from yesterday's shower; I worked some of it up in my hands and it left them red as vermillion.

I kept watching Black Butte, a huge, forbidding volcanic crater which is thrust up through the red desert like some cancer on the crust of the earth. Somewhere between it and the red cliffs to the east, where the desert breaks toward Moen Copie Wash, we were to find the ashes of Frank Sauerwein, the artist who painted pictures of the desert as long as his strength would permit, and dying asked that his ashes should be flung to the winds from some hill in his beloved land of mystery.

We came to the spot just before sundown, a sort of tiny basin running up to a deep cleft in the cliffs and strewn over with the haycock hills. On one of these, which had eroded away till it was only two or three feet above the basin floor, the ashes still lay in a slender line of white, though my guide and a companion had scattered them three months before.

All about was a tangle of the many-colored clay hills as if flung headlong, and from their wind-shaped bulk logs of petrified trees crawled out, or sprawled bare, or scattered their chips across the level spaces between. The ground was strewn with agates and shining iron pebbles and splinters of the jewelled wood glistened among the white of the unheeding ashes.

The great cliffs behind, rich-colored as anything that ever left the artist's brush, were monument fit for a king, but we carried broken lengths of the gorgeous wood and set them up to mark the thin white trail across the hillock.

July 26. We camped at some abandoned Navajo hogans on the bank of the Moen Copie Wash, which was roaring full of thin mud, rather than water. We had to settle it overnight before the horses could drink it and as there was no grass they had to be tied to a dead tree and given a stingy feed of the hay we had brought from Flagstaff, and plenty of the grain which made up the bulk of our load.

The water roared all night and the wind blew, but not hard enough to blow away the swarms of mosquitos. Sleeping on a sandbar has its mitigations, but sleeping on earth lately beaten solid by a mountain flood is like having a bed of iron. It didn't take me more than half the night to figure that our forefathers got up early not from any superior virtue, but because they slept on cord beds and husk mattresses, or on the floor with no more blankets than I had. Nobody had to call me in the morning and I didn't need a professor of anatomy to tell me how many bones I had.

This Moen Copie Wash follows a channel cut out by floods through the floor of a tiny valley which "canyons up" as it goes back into the red cliffs of the eastern plateau. The banks are many feet deep and straight as a wall and sleek and slippery as ice; but at the lower end there are a good many hundred acres of level land that will some day be cultivated. It would give farms for a lot of the Navajos who now come down and plant corn after the overflows and summer rains. There ought to be a chance to store water enough for all the land at moderate expense.

We went up along the right-hand bank of the wash to the Tuba crossing and found it gone and a perfect torrent of black water seeping over in a waterfall all ribbed with masses of froth and full of drift. There were moccasin tracks all along the bank so we knew the Indians were afraid to cross, but we found wagon tracks leading on up the right bank and followed them.

The sandy floor of the canyon was from a hundred yards to half a mile wide and back of it the cliffs rose again, the rich-toned blue and greenish and red clays seeming to be just the sheer, broken rim of the mesa above. The rains streaming down off this upper stretch of mesa had cut these clay cliffs into the most wonderful shapes, smoothed and glossed by the water; a great procession of draped figures seemed to move solemnly along the walls, hooded and mysterious, and remarkably suggestive of the relief sculptures in Egyptian temples.

We stopped for lunch under these "Watchers in the Desert" and a Navajo came along with two huge bales of wool wrapped in bright striped blankets and tied on either side of his small pony. He was as picturesque as an Arab, and as silent as one of the "Watchers"—till I opened up the camera and began to tell my guide how handsome he was. Then the bronze face relaxed into a regular "look pleasant" smile and he not only posed, but stayed for lunch and went with us to the next crossing.

Again the ford was gone and the Indians from their stick and mud hogans on the opposite bank waved us back. Some of them trotted off for the resident government farmer and he came on horseback and joined in the decision that it was not safe for us to cross. We sat with our handsome friend on the bank and watched the water get deeper as fresh floods came down from the mountains above; for us it meant camp in the sandhills with hungry horses and no feed, while acres of green cornfields reached up the other side of the canyon.

The sand was blowing in spiteful whirls as we made camp under the cliffs; however disappointed we were, we had "plenty of sand in our craws" —after supper. The horses gobbled their grain and champed and whinnied all night, and the mosquitos made the most of their chance and the coyotes howled cheerfully and a Navajo goat herd nearby added to the general hilarity.

JULY 27. The front-end of this day has gotten out of "hollering distance" from its close. The wash had the same Navajo grin on top when we went down to take observations after breakfast. We trailed around in a mile or two of sand-hills and young Grand Canyons broken down from the cliffs behind us, and found a ten-foot backbone that looked crossable for the empty wagon, though the official report from the masculine half of the expedition stated that it "looked like the top rafter on the roof of hell."

33

We hitched up and drove into a little hollow in the sand-hills as near the base of the "ridge-pole" as we could get; there we unloaded the wagon and drove back and around over that narrow bridge between no horse feed and the green pastures which we hoped were ahead. We slipped and slid and skidded and scooted, but we landed at the bottom right side up.

Then for hours in the broiling sun the combined expedition climbed over the hill packing the left-behind contents of the wagon up and down and reloading. There seemed to be enough stuff on the wrong side of the hill to load a battleship and the landscape ahead looked like one sand dune after another to the far side of creation—on our side of the wash.

It took hours to get through the sand to the point where we hoped to cross and there again the ford was gone and another roaring waterfall tearing along; but the wash had a rocky bottom upstream and after trying it with a single horse to be sure of all rock and no quicksand, we plunged in. At the steep opposite bank the tired horses couldn't make the pull and I scrambled over the wheel and up the muddy bank to ease them of my weight at least.

We landed at last in the green fields of corn and a friendly Moqui showed us a spring and tried to tell us the road up to the Indian school at Tuba. We got there at last, after pulling up a tough hill and through sand that took the last ginger out of the ponies. We had been following the tall green Lombardy poplars for three days and were almost as glad as the horses to get in.

JULY 28. Mr. Jeffrys, the Indian agent here, took me up to the school where I had the guest room and a bath tub at my service, and supper under a roof and off a table and unmixed with Moen Copie sand. The horses must rest and feed up, and as this is one of the early settlements of the Mormon people, I want to look it over.

This region is beautiful enough to pay for any hardship of getting into it, and without the floods the trip out would be fine all the way. It is a little less than a hundred miles from Flagstaff and looking that direction one may see the San Francisco peaks, with a wonderful reach of the Painted Desert in between.

The springs in this whole country have a curious way of coming out on top of the red sandstone cliffs or up on the plateaus on the eastern rim of the desert. The springs here are big enough to give water for a good deal of irrigation; one of them, which was located by Lot Smith, the old-time Mormon bishop, is believed to come from a great distance because, it is

34

said, small sticks and leaves and various objects are sometimes borne out in the flow from underground.

It is said that John D. Lee settled first in this region, while he was in hiding after the Mountain Meadow Massacre. Tuba has been a prosperous settlement, but a few years ago the government bought it for the Navajo and Moqui Indians and established the school.

The buildings are of the bright red sandstone, so red that I thought they were newly burned brick. The poplars and other trees and the fine orchard and garden make it a lovely spot and doubly so after the trip across. School is closed for the summer and there are few Indians about.

JULY 29. We went down to the little Moqui village today, about a mile and a half from Tuba and on a second terrace under the first wall of cliffs. This is a picture all by itself; the canyon walls here are perhaps a mile wide at the bottom and then terrace back in a succession of cliffs and sand-hills. Down in the bottom the fields of corn are as green as paint and the little peach orchards look like squares on a checkerboard. The little vegetable gardens with beans and squashes and onions are protected from the blowing sand by rows of arrow-weed and brush stuck in beside each row of plants, making a solid little shelter.

'Way across the deep red canyons the mesas and mountains seem to go on forever, and right down below on a little table of red rock the village sits like a toy fort with its stone houses and little, crooked streets. It is rather a new village and cleaner and more prosperous than those in the larger reservation sixty miles eastward.

As we drove down we met the friendly Moqui who showed us the spring yesterday, and he told us where to find the old "Queen" Maiwe, who seems to be highly regarded by her own people and by the school people too.

We found the old queen in quite a good house at the farther end of the village, where she could look down over the fields if she wanted to. She had a fine, bright, intelligent face that did not look so old, but her body was twisted with rheumatism and no doubt she is well into the eighties, as is said.

It seems that the Moquis had cultivated these fields long ago but the Navajos drove them all away, except Maiwe who was a strong and plucky young woman. She took a Navajo husband at one time, probably as a protection; when the Mormons came they were friendly to her and the Moquis began to come back. Recently the government has given them land and they have one of the most prosperous Moqui villages.

35

Maiwe owns the land on which the village stands; that may be why she has power, but it seems more her own superior wisdom. At one time she went to New Mexico to work and learn; she is to her people what some of our own fine women have been when courage and inspiration were needed.

In her comfortable house much corn was stored from last year's crop and the younger members of her family were grating roasting ears for bread and pounding the wheat just ripe into a coarse meal. She had baskets piled with the piki, the corn bread as thin as paper which is rolled up in little rolls and keeps a long time. She had baskets to sell and the whole place was well supplied with the simple things she used.

I wanted her picture and she offered to sit on a bench in the sun and let me take it for "four bits." When it was done she called a very old man who was spinning on a curious wooden spindle over at the back of the room. "My man," she said; "him picture, two bits!" The twinkle in her eyes showed that she thought she was getting the best of me even at half price, but I made them sit down side by side and got the queen and her "marked down" consort all in one shot.

I bought a basket which she had made for sifting the corn meal and got from her son a gourd rattle used in the religious dances. Then she showed me some drawings of the Katchinas made by her grandson, who attended the little school up on the hill. She seemed very proud of them and was glad to have me buy two, and said he was "much smart"—which seemed like grandmothers everywhere.

FOUR

The Echo Cliffs

Taking on new supplies at Preston's Trading Post at Tuba (the octagonal building is still used as a trading post), Sharlot Hall and her "guide" headed north on the road to Lee's Ferry. About six miles out they came to the small village of Moenave (spelled variously), another green oasis set against red sandstone cliffs and fed by bountiful springs. In hiding for complicity in the Mountain Meadows Massacre in 1857, John D. Lee, after first settling at Lee's Ferry, moved here where he lived for five months in 1873.

The Mormons, members of the Church of Jesus Christ of Latter-day Saints, bent upon colonizing the valleys of the Little Colorado, had opened the road to wagons from Utah south to Tuba City, Moenkopi and Moenave in 1873. Willow Springs, issuing from the base of cliffs a few miles north-west of Moenave, provided good water and offered an excellent camping place. Mormon colonists, as the Indians had done before them, often decorated the sandstone blocks nearby with their names, dates and assorted grafitti.

For sixty miles north of Willow Springs the road followed close to the base of the magnificent Echo Cliffs on the right, an unbroken, jagged escarpment in places running up to heights of over two thousand feet above the level. Meeting both Paiute and Navajo Indians along the way, the travelers watered at Government Wells near The Gap where a trading post was established later. Tanner's Well and Navajo Spring were both watering places on the old wagon road; today the traveler on U.S. Highway 89A may rest under shade trees at Navajo Spring and enjoy the good, sweet water piped down to the roadside from the spring a mile away at the base of the Echo Cliffs.

From Navajo Spring it was seven miles to Lee's Ferry. Dropping down over a surface alternately white and dark red, Sharlot and Al soon found that the right-hand cliffs had forced them out to a rim point overlooking the Colorado River. Many since have agreed with Sharlot Hall's words— the spot was "beautiful as it was wild and strange." Nearly two hundred feet directly below them, the Colorado, copper-colored, muddy and high with the spring run-off, flowed along like a crawling snake. There was much rain across the Colorado Plateau in 1911, as Sharlot's diary attests, and the Colorado was probably unusually high at the time. Ahead, on the other side of the river, the small settlement of Lee's Ferry, surrounded by green fields and orchards, stood out in welcome contrast to the red cliffs hemming it in on three sides.

In order to reach the ferry landing the travelers found they must drive over a mile-long dugway (built in 1898), a dizzy ride at best. (Sharlot refers to this road again on August 7.) On the left the river roared over a rapid below and the towering cliffs on the right seemed to lean out over them. Safely over the dugway, they shortly came to the ferry and Sharlot was put across the Colorado to her "Promised Land."

◂ℰ THE HORSES ARE RESTED and we have been buying things for the long trip to Fredonia, about two hundred miles away. From here on to Lee's Ferry we cross sandy country and no feed, so we have loaded up with grain and baled hay till there is hardly room in the wagon for the extra canned stuff. I have tried to get enough things that we shall not be hungry on the road, and yet not carry an extra pound. The roads are very bad, everyone says, and the ponies will do well if they can make it at all without unloading over the bad places.

It is between sixty and seventy miles from Tuba to the Ferry and only a few watering places between, and no houses or settlements. The agency doctor has gone to Flagstaff, but Mr. Jeffrys, the agent, has allowed me to get some extra medicines from the hospital drug room. I want to be sure of enough bandages and antiseptics in case of an accidental wound to ourselves or the horses, and of quinine and such things. I have permanganate of potash and other remedies for snake bites; this looks like a good rattlesnake country, and probably there are centipedes and tarantulas and scorpions.

The heat and the intense reflection of the sun on the sand plains and bright-colored cliffs has burned my face and eyes painfully and I have gotten a lot of witch hazel and talcum powder. The Navajos and Hopis here all seem to have sore eyes, as much from the glaring sun as from dirt and trachoma, I suspect, and I am careful how I handle their blankets and baskets. The Indian traders are trying to be careful, especially in handling the wool they buy, for the eye disease is very easily caught.

The trading post here is as interesting as the big post at Ganado. It is built of gray stone in the octagonal shape of a Navajo hogan; there are no windows in the sides, but on top where the opening in a hogan would be there are a great many windows set in an octagonal skylight. The entrance door carries out the hogan idea and the stock of goods is all disposed on shelves along the walls in plain sight, but behind a high counter which runs all around the room.

The Indians can see anything they want to buy but they cannot handle it, and as the clerk is behind the counter and his customers out in the octagonal court in the center of the room, with no chance to come back of the counter except through a locked gate too high to climb over, he and the goods would be safe in case of dispute. In fact, the trading post would make a fine fort and with a machine gun mounted in the skylight one or two white men could hold off the whole tribe.

The trader, S. S. Preston, has had a wonderfully varied experience among the Indians, having been a scout and packer with General Crook and a trader among the Navajos more than twenty years. There are few men living who have such accurate knowledge of Indian life and ways, and whose observations of Indian habits and character are so just and dependable. Mr. Preston is the man who captured Jim Parker, the train robber, and turned him over to Sheriffs Ruffner and Cameron at the crossing of the Little Colorado.

When we finally got the things that we were obliged to take packed into the wagon it was loaded to the very top; the rolls of bedding had to be pushed in right under the canvas top and the water bucket and halter ropes and hobbles for the horses tied on at the back, along with an extra bale of hay. It was so crowded that an extra box had to be tied on the side of the seat even, and I was glad to walk as much as possible, not only to spare the ponies my weight through the sand, which was a foot deep for miles at a stretch, but also to rest myself from the crowding and discomfort of riding in the wagon so packed and filled in every part.

The road out from Tuba has been dug out of the red sandstone cliffs that wall the Moen Copie Wash, and winds round and round the spurs and side canyons on the northern wall till finally it drops into the flat little valley at the bottom, where the sand begins to drag on the wheels and little farms are fenced in with brush and planted to corn and melons and beans, and now and then peach and plum trees.

From the road grade looking down, the fields look like green bits on a checker board, and far to the southwest the San Francisco Peaks wall the whole horizon with a blue bulk that seems like the broken quarter-section of a hemisphere set up on edge. We passed the little Presbyterian mission, seeming to shiver in its newness and smallness under the huge red cliffs; and away up in a high-lifted side canyon a circle of slender Lombardy poplars marked Moen Copie's spring, where the old chief of the name is said to have lived and died. The little shoulder of hillside on which they stood looked just like a churchyard in some old village, but the trees stood out strangely against the vivid red cliffs.

Bending away from the wash, around the curve of cliff-walled mesa, the Lee's Ferry road crossed great beds of sandstone eroded into fantastic shapes and covered with strange, burnt-looking black pebbles and fragments of lava-like rock, which on close examination has the texture of agate, in spite of being as full of little holes as a sponge. Many agates of coarse grade are scattered over the ground, some of them gorgeous in color.

The edge of the plateau is broken here into two terraces, the second one from the top being as much as a mile wide in places. At the widest part there is another small spring and the Mormon settlers had what must have been a good ranch just below it where water could be let out over the fields. The poplars and cottonwood trees still stand, most of them dead and desolate looking, and the wind has blown a huge dune of sand up out of the wash and drifted it many feet deep over the fields.

It is one of the curious features of this country that many mountainsides are covered with these strange sand dunes blown up to the very top and sometimes half way down the other side, by the wind, and rippled and lined as if the waves of some great tide had scarcely retreated from them. The sand, ground down by centuries from the vast red cliffs, is red and yellow and sometimes a soft rose color that seems impossible in such material.

Rounding another out-reaching spur of the long plateau, we saw a wedge-shaped canyon driven back into the huge rim, and far up against the ruddy walls the tallest poplars I have ever seen were massed and blended with the spires and towers of rock. This is Moen Avi, the farthest home and retreat of John D. Lee in the years following the awful Mountain Meadow Massacre, for which he was arrested and executed many years later.

It is like an eagle's nest; behind the great cliffs guard it from approach, and in front no one could come within many miles without being seen moving over the vast reach of bright, naked sand. A fine spring gushes down out of the red cliffs and still waters the orchard and a little strip of alfalfa and corn fields, but since the land was added to the Navajo Indian reservation and the Mormon settlers went away, everything has gone to ruin through neglect.

The orchard was a tangle of grape vines gone wild and climbing over the apple and peach trees; green apples and clusters of grapes mingled at the very top-most branches; under the plum trees the ripe fruit lay red and deep; the old-time garden was a mass of weeds, and the Indians were caring for nothing but some little patches of corn.

A Navajo hogan stood under a dead tree by the cliffs, but of the homes of the first settlers only some broken walls and crumbling old chimneys were left. The sand from the desert below is rolling in like some hungry sea, wave upon wave, and lies in ridges many feet deep just below the fields. Soon it will all be covered and only the lonely poplars will mark what was once a home in one of the wildest yet most strangely beautiful spots in the Southwest.

As we drove away I felt that I could almost turn Navajo for the chance to live in the midst of that silent, mystical, vividly colored, unearthly land. I could understand why the artist Sauerwein wanted his ashes to drift with the bright-hued sands up and down over those vast and glorious spaces.

Willow Springs, our night camp, is some ten miles beyond [Tuba City not] Moen Avi, and before we struck the road to it we heard the "bull-whackers" yelling and saw the yokes of oxen strung out on the road going back after the trail wagons which they had had to drop in the heavy sand. One of the men was riding bareback on a big dun ox, and he told us that the outfit had a hard time crossing Moen Copie Wash and one of the mule teams stuck in the quicksand and came near not getting out.

In about an hour we passed the lead wagons camped for dinner, and the men and cattle looked worn out and muddy. There was so little grass for the stock and the heat and deep sand made driving by day so hard that they laid up and let the cattle feed and drove at night. The cook was baking apple pies for dinner in a Dutch oven; they had gotten a lot of fruit from the Tuba orchard, and had several big ovens full of yeast bread almost ready to bake. The men had rustled sagebrush roots to make coals enough to go under and on top of the Dutch ovens, and the bitter smoke was about as good for the eyes as peeling onions.

Some two miles from Willow Springs we passed a scattered mass of great stones broken from the cliffs behind. They were quite smooth and covered with the greatest number of and the most perfect pictographs that I have ever seen. Evidently the little spring here has been permanent at some time, though now it only seeps a little in wet weather. A mile or so out in the desert we could see the ruins of a large pueblo on top of a detached hill and sherds of quite good pottery were strewn over the ground.

The Willow Spring itself is a fine big stream of clear water coming down out of a red sandstone canyon under the rim of the plateau, as all the water seems to do in this desert. It has a regular camping place for the Mormon emigrants and some of them had painted the name "Camp Windy" with the date of January, 1878, on the rocks.

About a hundred yards from our camp were the ruined walls of the Navajo trading post where Jim Parker, the train robber, stopped to get a supply of grub on his way north. He had been shot in the leg when he broke jail at Prescott and was pretty lame. The clerk recognized him and told Preston, the trader, who got a bunch of six or seven Navajos and trailed him up. Parker was so tired that he went to sleep and when he woke up at daylight he was looking into the business end of a ring of rifles.

The rocks all along the Willow Spring canyon have been carved with fine pictographs in great variety, as well as painted and scratched with the names of many travelers from the early seventies on. Away back in a tiny pocket, quite hidden from the outside, the Navajos have some hogans and little corn fields, but recent floods have almost scooped clean the whole canyon trough, and in a few years every bit of earth will be gone.

AUGUST 1. We are close up to the Echo Cliffs, a great wall of sandstone that runs north as far as I can see. Beginning at Moen Copie Wash, a curious series of these great ledges run north to the Big Colorado, notched and pinnacled like a cock's comb, and seeming to be the broken edges of the old plateau thrust sharply up through the sand beds of later erosion. Echo Cliffs must be about two thousand feet high, and the whole sheer front is banded so evenly with shadings of the stone from red to pinkish cream that the effect is remarkable.

Two sharply contrasting lines the whole length mark the edges of a ledge of greenish stone that seems to underlie the sandstone, and the walls are broken into deep wrinkled lines and clefts, with vast peaks like watch-towers and rows of boulders standing on the edge like uncouth monster animals with their heads high in the air.

We watered the horses at Government Wells, in the mouth of a deep canyon some two hundred yards away on the right-hand side of the road.

I had been watching all morning for it and was glad to find the dim road turning away to the shallow well which meant comfort to our tired horses.

Some ten miles beyond we came to the end of the Painted Desert, at least to the watershed between the Little and the Big Colorado Rivers. Here the curious hills of deep blue clay, said to contain about five dollars to the yard in flour gold, are piled in the wildest confusion and end in a big shouldering mountain, the Blue Hill, up which the ponies dragged the wagon with the greatest difficulty.

I walked close behind the wheels with as big a stone as I could carry to "chink up" when they stopped to rest, for the brake would hardly hold and the slippery clay, wet with a shower just past, made the hard work still harder. On top at last, I walked on through the low cedars and dwarf pinyon which covered the high trough of a valley into which we had risen.

Now at last there was grass, thick and green; the soil was no longer red clay, and though the gorgeous cliffs seemed to run on to the north pole on the right, the half-mile valley had ribs of rough white limestone on the left, all knotted up with box canyons that seemed to begin underfoot and end in a pocket in the cedars.

Down ahead blue twists of smoke were going up and a distant chorus of goats told that Indians were near. Some ponies were feeding in the cedars and an old squaw came out to get them. She shied off from the wagon, but a big apple, saved from the Moen Avi orchard, lured her in. She said she was a Pah-Ute and that there was water in a hole back in the cedars a mile beyond.

She looked like Age on a journey; the few rags that clung about her hardly covered her wrinkled body; her hair was grizzled white and matted and wild, and her dull eyes looked like bits of agate in the gnarled old face that had little human about it. She begged for bread but the wagon was so piled full of things that I could not get at the grub box till we went into camp.

We made camp about a mile on in the cedars and the guide went off with the horses to find the water hole. I made a fire and began supper and the smoke had hardly gotten above the tree tops when two thin little Pah-Ute girls about six and eight raced up to beg, crying "bis-ke, bis-ke." They were naked except for a wisp of flour sack over the back of one and the collar and some ragged strips of a shirt on the other, and their thin little bodies looked like hard times on the range.

I gave them each an apple and some bread and before they had gone some young men raced up on their ponies, almost running into the fire. They were well dressed with leggings and bright shirts, and had beautiful blankets and some silver trinkets. They fingered over the sacks of grain on the ground and started for the grub box, demanding bread in no very gentle tones.

I will feed the children and the old people, but we are more than a hundred miles from supplies on ahead and I am not going to waste food on "fat and sassy" young Indians, so I told them to get out of camp. They didn't go with very good grace, but they saw I had a gun handy and they finally got on their ponies and galloped off.

A girl of ten or twelve soon crept up to the fire and begged for bread. She spoke some English and said she had been at the Tuba school. The poor little thing was blind in one eye from some acute disease, and the other eye was inflamed. She looked sick and pitiful and I was glad to feed her and give her some witch hazel.

A man came in later begging bread, and when it was given to him did not touch a bite but said he wanted it for his sick child over at the camp. I was glad to give him what I could and he seemed so grateful I would have been glad to make it more. These Indians mostly live across the Colorado River and come in here with their goats and ponies in the summer when the rains have made grass. They had some poor little corn fields in the middle of the valley, fenced with cedar logs, but the corn was just in tassel and they were living on grass seeds and a little goat meat.

We are camped in the southern end of Echo Cliff Valley; a narrow trough running northward as far as I can see. On the right-hand side the great wall of Echo Cliffs runs away into the distance like a broken section of the Grand Canyon; sheer faces of sandstone dropping down in stairs and terraces and buttressed by peaks whose huge size is lost in the greatness of the whole.

The coloring is like a Scotch tartan in rusty red brown and cream, with the big dyke of green trapstone slanting along the bottom, like a shoulder sash.

The little cedars on the ledges look like ornamental plants and a dark fringe of piñon hangs over the top of the farthest cliff line.

On the left low hills of red and white sandstone are broken by dozens of deep, short canyons and covered with scrubby cedar and piñon.

The grass is tall and green and the herds of goats and sheep are too lazy and full to feed. All along the middle of the valley are patches of corn in tassel; planted in low places that flood when it rains and fenced around by dead logs like a brush pile on end.

We met some Indian women and children coming out of a field with their arms full of green stalks. They were chewing it as southern darkeys chew sugar cane. Some of them had sore eyes and begged for medicine. They were afraid of the camera and the children began to run when it was pointed at them.

A mile or so further on I saw a summer hogan built of cedar boughs and open at the top. It hardly turned the sun and wind, but some distance away I found a very well built winter hogan. A large circle had been cleared in the forest and the earth removed over a place some fifteen feet in diameter, and a foot deep. The cedar logs had been stripped clean of bark and laid up very cleverly in an octagon room curving gracefully to the dome-shaped roof with a round smoke-hole in the middle. The roof poles were woven together almost as neatly as a basket and gave an effect of great beauty. The whole interior was beautiful, the smooth, creamy yellow logs splashed with sunshine from door and roof hole, and fragrant with spicy cedar odors.

Outside the red earth was banked up to the very top till not a log showed; the little round red mound might have been one of the "Haystack Hills" in the Painted Desert. The cooking ashes were out under the trees and most of the work had been done there instead of in the house.

The valley is a very Indian paradise—wood and grass and shelter and little corn-field spots all along—but water is scarce except in the rainy season and the snow must fall deep in the winter.

Near the upper end of the valley where the hills on the left hand run into a regular canyon wall we watered the horses at Tanner's Well. It is a pool scraped out a few feet deep so the horses could walk down an incline to the water, which is bitter with some mineral which we were told is arsenic. The well looked like a corner of Palestine and there were some ruins of small stone houses near and old, forgotten names scratched on the cliffs and boulders. The Mormon emigrants had made many a camp here and before them some prehistoric people had left figures scratched on the same cliffs.

Beyond the well we crossed a rough divide and turned down toward the Colorado River. Far across the rim the Pah-reah [Paria] Plateau stood huge and gorgeously colored. Our road went down sharply over a series of rough and rocky terraces, many little shoulder-like mesas jammed close together.

The great cliffs on the right grew more and more fantastic, broken and sand-carved into weird and gloomy shapes like waiting monsters—the mesa-ridges over which the road wound were cloaked with red sand deep and soft as wool on the back of a dirty sheep and the grass and shrubs dwindled away to parched wisps of last year's growth.

The hay we had carried was long since gone and the grain low; the water keg was empty, too, and the horses moved along wearily as if afraid of the strange, wild country we had brought them to.

We were driving to reach Navajo Spring off somewhere in a side-canyon to the right but the dark came down so fast we had to give up and make a dry camp.

This night I shall never forget; the wind blew and howled down out of the Echo Cliff peaks like a wild beast and beat the sand into everything. The horses tramped around the wagon too hungry and thirsty to rest, and I ached all over from the walking and could not sleep.

Toward morning the poor horses broke away and wandered over the hills. At daybreak the guide followed their tracks—no hard thing to do for they sank into the sand at every step.

August 3. Poor Mack and Dan got into camp long after I had breakfast ready; they had sighted some wild burros and tried to follow them over the side canyons to the river. They came near to balking on the first pull and I walked on ahead as usual to save them my weight in the wagon.

We found the Navajo Spring in a side canyon more than a mile from the road where the green top of a willow tree shone like a flag of welcome against the rusty cliffs.

Going on we met the Navajo mail carrier on a pony hardly bigger than an antelope and loaded with mail bags, camp outfit, and a big roll of tanned buckskins till only its ears stuck out over the pack. Skirting round the wagon the Navajo came to my side and asked if "Char-lot Missie" was there —having gotten that much of my name from some tribesman at Tuba probably. He said the people at Lee's Ferry were looking for me.

We dropped down over a lot of hills that seemed made out of all the scrapings of the Painted Desert and saw a big copper line like a badly twisted snake crawling along below with the greenest fields I ever saw beyond it and the reddest cliffs behind them.

The road looked as if it had been cut out of the red clay mountains with a pocket knife; sometimes it hung out over the river so we seemed sliding into the muddy current and again the cliffs above hung over till one grew dizzy to look. It was as beautiful as it was wild and strange and I doubt if there is a wilder, stranger spot in the Southwest. The fields that John D. Lee had planted were green under the beetling walls of the Vermillion Cliffs and the house he had built showed through the orchard he had grown from seeds.

But the quarter mile of liquid-copper river was between and a scrap of board beside the road said in pencil, "Fire a gun here if you want to cross."

As we reached the bank where the road ended in a sort of beaver slide down to the edge of the water, a gasoline boat about as big as a bath tub began to crawl across like a water bug.

It drew up on our bank and I and the camera and a suit case were loaded in and away the little vessel slid into the copper-red, swirling water and presently pulled again to shore and I jumped out on the southern edge of my Promised Land—in the "Arizona Strip" at last.

FIVE

Lee's Ferry

Lee's Ferry was a natural, if difficult crossing of the Colorado River. It was the only place above the mouth of Grand Canyon, 279 miles distant, where the river could even be reached on both sides by wheeled vehicles. And there were no better crossings for an equal distance upstream. At Lee's Ferry the Colorado dramatically breaks through the Echo Cliffs, leaving Glen Canyon behind. Then it sweeps out into the open for about two miles before being swallowed by Marble Canyon. This was an important cross-roads and Sharlot Hall and Al Doyle spent six days at the ferry, resting, soaking up history, admiring the magnificent scenery on all sides, and learning what they could about travel conditions ahead.

From her unpublished diary we learn that Sharlot at Lee's Ferry composed "The Squaw Man," one of her better known poems. In it the white man laments his marriage to the Indian woman and the birth of their half-breed child. He longs too late for the girl of his boyhood's love. The theme was probably suggested by a mixed marriage encountered the year before when she traveled deep into the Navajo country. The poem was finished on Saturday and that evening some of the boys from the mine came over to Lee's ranch to talk and listen to music supplied by a gramophone. We note also that Sharlot had found room in the wagon for Dellenbaugh's Romance of the Colorado River *and now in the pleasant shade of Lee's spreading pear tree she read that in 1776 the two Spanish friars, Dominguez and Escalante, were the first white men to reach the place. Mormon explorers came in 1858. John Wesley Powell on his first traverse of the Colorado stopped here briefly in 1869 and members (including Dellenbaugh) of Powell's second expedition spent some time here in 1871 and 1872.*

In December, 1871 (not 1869), while Powell's men were absent, John D. Lee arrived to found the first settlement. Excommunicated by the Mormon

Church and exiled to the spot, he put up a log cabin or two, planted crops and orchards along the lower banks of the Paria River, a small desert stream coming into the Colorado on the right side.

Lee operated a ferry of sorts, using first the Nellie Powell, *a boat (the one to which Sharlot refers, a fragment of which may be seen at the visitor center at Grand Canyon) abandoned by Powell on his second expedition. Regular ferry service was not begun until 1873 after Lee had gone to live at Moenave and other places, fearing arrest for participating in the Mountain Meadows massacre. He was eventually arrested, tried by jury, and sentenced to death in 1877. Sharlot undoubtedly refers to Emma Lee, one of John D's several wives, who stayed on after his arrest to run the ferry and maintain the home at Lee's Ferry which she called "Lonely Dell." After Lee's death ownership of the ferry passed to the Mormon Church, then to the Grand Canyon Cattle Company, and finally to Coconino County, Arizona, who operated it until 1928. The present highway bridge across the Colorado six miles downstream was completed in 1929 and this put Lee's Ferry out of business and the historic spot soon slid into oblivion.*

But in 1911, Sharlot Hall found the place alive with activity. A small mining boom was under way. The year before Charles H. Spencer, miner and promoter, had come to Lee's Ferry to try his hand at recovering gold from the nearby Chinle shales and from the sands of the Colorado riverbed. For two and a half years Spencer labored to save enough gold to make a go of it. He hauled in boats, set up a hydraulic operation, built trails, and opened coal mines to operate heavy steam-powered equipment. But the enterprise was a failure and he shut down in 1913.

Actually there were two ferry crossings at Lee's Ferry and Sharlot mentions Spencer's use of them. The upper crossing, and the safest, was reached by the dugway which she and Al Doyle had taken. The lower crossing, reached by a steep grade on the left side, avoided the dugway but it was more hazardous.

Anxious to report any resource development on the Arizona Strip, Sharlot Hall talked at length with Spencer, whose outfit had helped her cross the Little Colorado, and learned that Glen Canyon above Lee's Ferry and the tributary canyon of the San Juan had been prospected for gold for years (but only for twenty-eight, not fifty, years). Spencer himself previously had engaged in an unsuccessful mining venture on the San Juan River. In fact very few ever made wages in the Colorado River placers; the gold, as Sharlot reports, was just too fine to save by any method. Spencer's yarn about his "discovery that this 'white iron' is really free quicksilver" is one

*of the better bits of Colorado River folklore and we may thank Sharlot Hall
for capturing it in print.*

*On August 8 Sharlot was treated to a boat ride up into Glen (not Echo,
though this may have been a name in local usage at the time) Canyon, a
name given by John Wesley Powell. One of the "glens" was a spot he called
"Music Temple," seventy-five miles upstream and now covered by Lake
Powell, where some of his party inscribed their names. Although the Colorado in Glen Canyon was a placid stream many lives have been lost to its
waters. Sharlot Hall quickly sensed the power of the river when she wrote
"Death sits mighty close to the bank here."*

⊷§ AUGUST 4. We are in camp under a giant pear tree planted by John
D. Lee; my tent is under one side of the wide branches and the wagon
under the other. The ponies must rest and I want to see the mine as well as
this historic old place.

Since about 1858 the Mormons have known this crossing of the Colorado
and Lee came here to live about 1869. He was here when Major Powell
came down the river on his second trip; a boat in the yard here is said to
be one of Powell's boats but I think this must be a mistake.

There is a little log cabin nearby which was the first house Lee built.
Some of the logs in it show that they were originally used in some sort of
raft or rude ferryboat, either here or higher up the river.

When Lee's wife stayed here alone as she did much of the time the
Navajo Indians often crossed here and they were not always friendly. A
party of them came one night and built their camp fire in the yard and
Mrs. Lee understood enough of their talk to know she was in danger.
Brave woman as she was, she knew she must overawe them and she
took her little children and went out and spread a bed near the fire in
the midst of the hostile camp and stayed there till morning. When the
Navajos rode away they called her a brave woman and said she should
be safe in the future.

AUGUST 5. The gold mining camp here is the most interesting one I have
ever seen, and as I grew up in a placer mining region and understand the
ways of working, I have been out over the plant all day.

The river cuts through great hills of clay from here all the way up to the
San Juan, 150 miles away. At a distance the cliffs and peaks look like the
sandstone, red and brown and greenish gray or slate blue, but they are a
sort of dried silt like the clay hills of the Painted Desert. This clay assays

from fifty cents to five dollars a cubic yard in gold and the prospecting by the present company has been largely by assay as the gold is flour fine and can very seldom be caught in panning.

This whole region from the San Juan River down to the head of Marble Canyon, some miles below the ferry, has been prospected for fifty years and a good deal of coarse placer gold taken out in places, but no large deposit was ever found.

John D. Lee and later Warren E. Johnson, who took charge of the ferry at Lee's death, bought gold dust from the Navajos and may have known places where it was found in small quantities, but the Indians have always refused to tell the region where they get the coarse gold and nuggets. Various outfits have tried to work the gravel and sand in the river bottom with dredges and the existence of "pay dirt" has been proven but none of the work has yielded a profitable return.

For years the placer miners in the San Juan region contended with a substance which they called "white iron" and which they said carried away the flour gold out of the pan or sluices so they could not save wages.

After years of work in the San Juan the manager of the present Lee's Ferry company, who is a practical mining man of very wide experience, made the discovery that this "white iron" is really free quicksilver. Such a thing as quicksilver mingled with the clays of a region where no cinnabar ore is found has never been known before, and mineralogists declared it could not be true. Mr. Spencer has kept on with his experiments, till at present time he is washing out and saving a tank, sixty pounds, of quicksilver in every twelve hours run of the small test plant in operation here. Mining men from all parts of the world and some eminent mineralogists have made the long journey over the desert to see this remarkable deposit of clays and the presence of the quicksilver is no longer questioned. The banks of clay are washed down by a hydraulic process with water pumped from the river. The clay melts away rapidly under water and a great quantity of it can be put through the sluice boxes in a day.

There is no "tailings" or waste except some clay nodules from the size of a quail's egg up to a man's fist; no boulder, no adobe balls as in Central Arizona placer mines—the whole mountain could be piped through a twelve-inch string of boxes.

Sluice box amalgamation is not possible, however, with this clay, so no riffles are used in the boxes, which serve only to carry the dirt to an amalgamator which is the special invention of Mr. Spencer and his associates and combines such points of the Pierce and other machines as meet the needs of this particular clay formation.

The whole question in all this region has been how to save the flour gold —for it has been certain for years that it existed in paying quantities, if some method could be invented to save it. The present plant is temporary and experimental, the boxes being small, but a great quantity of machinery is waiting here to be installed at once and by the first of November a large quantity of clay will be handled, both here and at the camp forty miles higher up the river.

At present all machinery and supplies are brought either from Flagstaff, on the Santa Fe railroad, or from Marysvale, Utah, by ox team, a haul in either case of 150 miles over very bad roads and entirely unsettled country. The machinery received by way of Flagstaff and now out in the Painted Desert on the ox wagons which we passed, is to be towed up the river on flat boats by the thirty-horsepower gasoline launch on the lead wagon and by two small gasoline boats already here.

A fifty-horsepower steamboat is being built in sections in San Francisco and will be brought down from Marysvale, Utah, and launched at the Pahreah camp in November. There is a fine deposit of coal about twenty miles up the river and the steamboat will deliver it at both camps for use of the engines that pump for the hydraulic works.

AUGUST 7. The ox teams were seen this morning just on the divide at the head of the long "dug way" that winds around the clay cliffs along the river to the ferry.

This is a wonderful bit of road building; the old Mormon road went lower down but the river washed it away and the new road is slashed and carved out along places where it would make an eagle dizzy to fly; yet the work has been done so well that at least one automobile has come in over these terrific grades.

I went across the river again in the little toy gasoline boat and climbed the grade to see the big wagons pass. The cattle were lean and sore and caked with sweat and dust, and the men looked like black, hollow-eyed ghosts. They had been held up by the floods, bogged in quicksand, harassed by heat, and had travelled by night for the most part to let the cattle feed and rest in the heat of mid-day.

The new gasoline boat was too long to go round the sharp turns of the "dug way"; it was unloaded and launched at the foot of the grade and came up over the half mile of rapids like a seabird.

The heat along the grade was great and the cattle were ready to drop when they got the wagons to the river at the ferry. They were unyoked and will be crossed on the ferryboat, leaving the wagons to be loaded on the barge for the up-river trip.

One tired animal got down the bank and tried to swim over; the current caught him and he was sucked under in spite of his strongest struggles, and was never seen again. A wagon and team and two men were lost here in the spring by the tipping of the ferryboat. This wild river takes its toll every few months; the very waves as they pass look fierce and tameless and hungry.

AUGUST 8. They are loading the wagons on the barges today and will tow up the river tonight. One of the Johnson boys, who almost grew up on the river, took me a long way up into Echo Canyon in a rowboat and we floated back after dusk. The canyon here is about 1,500 feet sheer wall, then terraced back in great mountains. The color is dark, deep red and one has to "look twice" to see the sky. The whirlpools and eddys caught us and pulled at the boat like some big hand under the water running along like copper-colored oil.

It was some miles up this canyon that two of Powell's men, who were later lost, left their names on the cliffs.

The current was fierce as we came down. It was this same wild current that Father Escalante feared to cross in 1776; he turned back after coming down and riding into the river twice. I don't blame him. Death sits mighty close to the bank here.

SIX

Buffalo Country

On August 9 Sharlot Hall and Al Doyle pulled out for Fredonia, well over eighty rough miles ahead. Skirting the great Vermilion Cliffs of the Paria Plateau on the right their route was very close to the present Highway 89A. For the first sixteen miles the cliffs, "Wilder and grander" than anything they had seen so far, towered a full three thousand feet directly above the road. Sharlot commented on the huge balanced rocks one may see alongside the highway from Marble Canyon to Lee's Ferry and at the crossing of Soap Creek on Highway 89A where the Cliff Dwellers Lodge was built at a later day.

Camp for the night was in House Rock Valley at Jacob's Pools, a spring discovered by the Mormon pioneer Jacob Hamblin and occupied for a time by John D. Lee. To reach the spring the travelers crossed miles of red sand. What an incongruous sight in that "weird red landscape" to see a line of black buffalo trailing to water!

In 1906 E. F. "Buffalo" Jones and James T. "Uncle Jim" Owens had brought bison to House Rock Valley, a wide and open expanse between the straight-walled Paria Plateau and the rounded eastern slopes of the Kaibab Plateau, where they bred the wild animals with domestic cattle. Some hybrid animals—"cattalo"—were produced but the experiment was not a commercial success. Buffalo, now under state control, still roam on a range in the southern extremity of House Rock Valley.

Camp for the second night after leaving Lee's Ferry was made under the roof of the main building at House Rock Ranch—still to be seen by Highway 89A at the base of the Kaibab Plateau—the one-time headquarters of John W. Young, one of the more aggressive entrepreneurs of northern Arizona. Next day our travelers proceeded north up the valley about five miles to House Rock Spring, a major watering place on the pioneer wagon

road between Utah and Arizona. Near this spot two large blocks of sand-
stone had fallen together in such a way as to form a crude shelter. Men had
used it for that purpose and someone had written on the blocks in char-
coal, "Rock House Hotel." The spring was known by its proximity to the
house rock, hence House Rock Spring. The name, fixed on the maps by the
Powell Survey, was extended to the valley and the ranch.

House Rock Valley pinches out above the spring a few miles and follow-
ing a well-established track Sharlot and her guide began the steep climb
up the eastern slope of the Kaibab Plateau, also known at the time as the
Buckskin Mountain, or Mountains. Beautiful vistas over the intricately
eroded sandstone country to the north and east were cut off when they
entered the heavy piñon forest on top of the Kaibab, 6500 feet in elevation.
But six miles put them through the forest and they jolted down over the
rough western slope. Ahead they could see well over fifty miles to the west
over the Arizona Strip, almost "to the end of things." On the north the
Vermilion Cliffs were visible just over the line in Utah. Reaching a nearly
dry spring, which was most likely a watering place known as Navajo Wells,
the tired travelers called it a day.

◄§ AUGUST 9. We have gotten all the information about the road to
Fredonia that the people here can give us; it is sandy in long stretches and
very rough over the Buckskin Mountains, and we shall find few watering
places. It follows the right bank of the river for several miles, keeping
under the shadow of the Vermillion Cliffs.

This great cliff wall which is the southern and western rim of the Pahreah [Paria] Plateau is wilder and grander than anything we have seen so
far. The upper cliffs are broken into many-toothed turrets and spurs like
long fangs against the sky and their dark iron-rust color all blotched and
smeared with lighter splashes makes the blue of the air seem purple.

From their base the clay hills roll down, pitted with smooth boulders
like the wash of a hundred layers of sea beach. Sometimes they lie in long
walls—regular as if laid up by hand. Again erosion has cut away the clay
and the huge stones, polished and worn into fantastic shapes, are flung
over the little terraces above the river in utter confusion. Erosion is working rapidly here—the whole clay base of the cliffs seems slipping into
the river.

The road skirted little gullies and wound among the strange stones—
boulders of many tons were balanced on slender necks of clay like acrobats.
One seemed a big skull and in the deep eye-sockets a desert rat had made

its nest; one looked like a "Teddy bear" and on top a red cactus was blooming. Some had big hollows underneath where travellers had found shelter and many were written over with black paint or axle grease with names and with directions about roads and water.

We found water at Soap Creek, about sixteen miles from the Ferry, a little stream with the peculiar clearness which alkali gives, flowing through a deep gash of a gully in a soapy blue clay.

All about us [the eroded rocks?] seemed [like?] the men of a dead land. We dragged through beds of deep sand or bumped over boulders and ribs of rock and through endless gullies where the road was washed away and the wagon rocked and reeled and all but toppled over.

The very lizards that darted away from me as I walked ahead of the wagon were gray and old looking.

The road bent away from the river, almost north, into the mouth of Rock House Valley, which lies like a shallow trough between the ragged red wall of the Vermillion Cliffs and the white limestone whaleback foothills of the Kaibab Plateau.

Five miles more of sandy road—the ponies almost too tired to move— then we found big trails leading to the right and knew there was water somewhere at the base of the cliffs.

The guide was walking, trying to find a wagon road among the trails. I was driving and watching a gorgeous red sunset over the sand-hills. Suddenly a line of huge black animals came over the hills, outlined black against the sunset clouds—big-humped and shaggy-maned and moving lazily down the trail.

I could have believed them the monster creatures of some moon-world, so wild and strange they looked in that weird red landscape.

Then I remembered the buffalo herd of which we had been told—part of the lessening remnant of those great herds of the plains. I remembered the buffalo calves that my father captured when I was a little child on the edge of that "buffalo grass country."

Six little red calves were trotting and capering along the trail beside their mothers—all curious about the moving, white-topped wagon and white horses that were invading their feeding grounds.

August 10. We camped last night in a little nest of clay hills and sand washes so covered with petrified wood that it looked like an old logging camp; the stumps and logs stuck out of the hillsides and the splintered wood lay all over the ground—some of it so natural in color and grain that

56

I had to look twice before I knew it wouldn't do for the breakfast fire.

I had seen petrified wood a hundred miles south of the Holbrook forests and since leaving the Little Colorado River near Black Falls we have found new forests or single logs every few days. This wood is not agatized as beautifully as that in the better known forests but it is very curious and the trees have been fully as large.

Some of the wood looks just like worm-eaten cottonwood, having holes in it and the dull color of dry wood.

There had been showers of rain all night long, and the wet logs stood out clear and clean, black or gray or dull blue. The ground is strewn with beautiful agates and the same curious soapy clay that we found in the Painted Desert shows up here. The forests seem never far from this curious clay, usually the trees are half buried in it; it washes easily in the rain and the little hillocks are eroded into fantastic shapes.

Before daylight I saw big dark shapes moving along the little rise above the camp; the buffalo were feeding across to the sheltered canyon, stopping to look down at us and especially at the white ponies. At sunrise I loaded up the camera and started to get some pictures; the herd stopped and watched me as I came nearer and presently began to switch their short tails and sniff the air and paw a little—striking all sorts of beautiful poses if there had been light enough for a shot.

The best one in the herd was a fine old bull, a pure buffalo, and as he pawed and bellowed I felt like cursing the clouds overhead. A gust of rain swept down in their faces and I had to shut up the camera under my raincoat and take it to camp.

I wanted to see the herd "close to" so after we harnessed up and the rain was pouring in torrents I rolled up in a Navajo blanket and crawled up a gully very close to the old king and his band. There were several half and quarter breeds, the "cattalo" which I had heard of but never seen before— buffalo crossed on Galloway cattle. They are lighter and smaller than the full bloods, with sharper horns and without the beautiful manes. The little calves were shining and fat and full of play as any calf on a rainy morning.

The rain kept on pouring and we drove up the Rock House Valley with the Vermillion Cliffs red as wet blood under the rain on the left [right, actually] and the great, gray shoulder of the Kaibab Plateau, or Buckskin Mountains, to the right [left], all twisted and wrinkled with canyons like a dried rawhide.

Streaks of green forest ran down the canyons and taller pines showed along the distant skyline. This valley is as wild and remote as some valley

57

on the moon; it lies in a shallow curve between the two great plateaus, with ridges of sand running out across it like fingers. Just now the bottom is green as paint with the crop of weeds and grass following the abundant summer rains.

The wagon cover was leaking and my raincoat holding puddles of water in every fold when we dragged over a higher sand-ridge and I saw a little red sandstone house as prim and trim looking as any farmhouse, standing on the edge of that wild reach of Nowhere.

I had a moment's hope of seeing somebody, man or woman, who could tell us whether we were on the right road and how far it was to Fredonia but the little place was deserted. We went in at the open back door and found a big fireplace and dry wood enough to start a fire; some old traps littered the floor and a lizard ran up the wall in fright but the dry, warm room seemed like a palace to me.

After I had cooked dinner and we had unloaded the wagon and spread all the wet things out along the fence to dry I amused myself by reading the pencil scrawls all over the walls. Evidently this little house had sheltered many a weary and storm-beaten traveller and their gratitude was written on the walls—along with some flings at the country itself. I copied a lot into my notebook.

Some of the guests had left dates, as one: "Oct. 4, 1908. A heavy snow storm on old Buckskin on the 2nd—very grateful for Mr. House, especially for Mr. Fireplace. Gracia and adios. Wind blowing like hell."

Another, probably a summer visitor, had left his plaint: "When you are travelling through the sandy deserts of Arizona most famished for water and team give out always thank the man that put up the little rock house and watering place. A Missouri Puke bound for Oregon; and I'll keep going. I may be crazy but I haint no fool."

A cowboy had left a pencil sketch of a limp-looking man on horseback and this sorrowful complaint: "Crossed the sand desert in a sand storm. Trappers from Coyote ranch landed here in the night. Gee! what a lonesome place! Everything looks dreary; everything looks weary,—to hell with this windy hole!"

Another brief sojourner had written on the door: "All the bad country in the U.S. was put together and they called it Arizona."

I was more inclined to echo the ones who had written "Thanks Little House; thanks Mr. Fireplace; thank you Mr. Man that built this place."

It was built by John W. Young, a son of President Brigham Young, and this valley was once stocked with cattle owned by a Mormon church com-

58

pany. Jacob Hamblin, the great Mormon explorer, came down through this valley many times from the early sixties to the late seventies and marked out the road over which his people travelled to colonize in the Little Colorado River region.

AUGUST 11. Headed up the Rock House Valley this morning; it must be twenty-five miles wide here and probably fifty long as it runs down to the rim of Marble Canyon through which the Colorado flows below Lee's Ferry. We can still see away to the southwest [southeast] where the huge walls of the Grand Canyon proper begin.

Our road follows close to the foot of the Vermillion Cliffs on the right-hand side of the valley. They are so wonderful that I can hardly take my eyes off them, probably 2,000 feet high and carved by wind and storm into peaks and facades as grand as Hawthorne's "Great Stone Face." They are the brightest and deepest red of anything in the way of earth that I have ever seen and a purple mist fills all the little clefts and canyons.

The water in this country all seems to break out in this red sandstone and often high up above the valley. The water at the little stone house is piped down out of a canyon into a dirt reservoir covering about half an acre. This has been a great cattle country and the whole valley is furrowed with old trails; the range has evidently been overstocked for most of the grass is gone and weeds grow in its place as farther south in Arizona.

This valley would make a fine farming country and I think water could be developed or stored but at present the springs are owned by a cattle company whose summer ranch we can see over across the valley at the foot of the Buckskin Plateau.

We came this evening in the midst of another deluge of rain to Jacob Hamblin's "Rock House Hotel" which gave the valley its name. It is just a big block of sandstone fallen from the cliff and looking more or less house-like, with a cave in the side which served to shelter Hamblin and his companions in their first exploring trip. One of them took a piece of charred wood from the camp fire and wrote "Rock House Hotel" on the front of the rock before they went on and the valley has borne the name for years.

The spring flows out from a seam in the sandstone and is piped into water boxes for the cattle. The rock erosion along the low cliffs here is the most remarkable that I have ever seen. Just above the rock hotel a huge frog crouches as if just ready to leap into the little valley and a menagerie of queer animals seems to be lined up along the broken red rimrock.

During the afternoon we came into a valley like a narrow box between

59

the red sandstone edge of the Pahreah [Paria] Plateau and the white lime-stone foothills of the Kaibab. This valley rose rapidly and it was clear that we would soon say goodbye to House Rock. I walked ahead as usual and presently found a lot of prehistoric Indian ruins: the low walls of a dozen or more houses and scattered fragments of pottery and a few arrowheads. This is a piñon pine country and no doubt the people of the past came to gather nuts, just as the Pah-Utes do now.

Now we had the most tremendous mountain panorama before us; we were climbing every hour and could look out over the top of the Pahreah Plateau on the right hand—a semi-mesa covered in wildest confusion with cones and saw-toothed peaks of rich-tinted sandstone and overgrown with cedar and piñon trees. The red land seemed to grow redder every mile and the sunset brought masses of purple and gold in the sky and deep smoke-drifts of lavender haze in the canyons.

Straight ahead but far to the northeast rose snow-covered peaks all streaked with gorgeous color at the base and in between the earth seemed slashed into a huge net of rainbow-colored canyons with the low green forest sparsely covering the ridges between.

To the left the Buckskin Mountains looked like a big land tortoise with a shell of steel gray limestone up which we could see tomorrow's road winding in dizzy fashion.

Some cattle came near the camp and we thought it seemed friendly to see them, knowing that the nearest human being must be a hundred miles away.

AUGUST 12. This morning we have filled the water barrel and every can-teen for now we must climb the whole length of the Kaibab without water. The next spring is clear at the foot of the mountain on the further side and the horses will suffer at the best we can do for them. It is about forty-five miles across, we were told at the Ferry.

Now the huge ranges to the northeast grow more wild and high and beautiful; I have walked all morning, it is all the ponies can do to pull the wagon; they sweat and puff and their feet slip on the smooth limestone; I could not bear to stay in the wagon no matter how tired I felt.

Now we are in the gray sage country and the air is pungent with its bitter scent; it drowns the piñon balsam and the quinine bush that is in full blossom. It must be the chief food of the cattle for there is almost no grass. We did find enough at noon for the horses and gave them a bucket of water each.

I started out again after noon walking through the forest; the road wound in and out among the low trees and seemed lost half the time. This is a pure limestone country and the surface stone is as rough and broken and clinker-like as if it had been baked in an oven.

We rounded the turtle back about four o'clock and looked down over a valley that seemed to reach east and west to the end of things—on the north it was walled in by more red cliffs like the House Rock. The road down off the edge was a regular limestone stairway and the wagon rolled and rocked and skidded behind the sweating ponies, while I walked alongside with as big a stone as I could carry to chunk up under the wheels when they stopped to rest.

The Mormon colonists who travelled this road certainly had grit when they started and got enough more to last the rest of their lives on the road. The valley was a sand bed a foot deep and after dragging through it till the ponies seemed ready to fall we came up to the promised spring and found it dry and a band of lowing cattle fighting over the damp earth and chewing the banks.

We managed to start a drip of water by running the shovel handle back between the ledges of limestone and caught this in a tin cup till we had enough to wash out the horses' mouths and help them a little.

SEVEN

Fredonia and the Mormons

Green, its streets lined with poplars, the Mormon village of Fredonia was located on the left bank of Kanab Creek just three and a half miles from the Arizona boundary. Founded in the 1880's, it was an offshoot of the older town of Kanab located upstream seven miles in Utah. It was an oasis in a red desert and our limping travelers found it a welcome sight. In her diary Sharlot wrote that she found a room with the Jensens, Danish people, who for dinner that night set out a delicious chicken stew.

Sharlot mentions the "Pah-Ute country." In 1866, Congress lopped off the extreme northwestern part of Arizona Territory and gave it to Nevada. This area—called by Arizona historians the "Lost County of Pahute"—had been colonized previously by the Mormons. When Nevada laid a heavy tax burden on them, they preferred to move back to Utah rather than pay. Some of their number, as Sharlot found out, returned to live in Arizona—in Fredonia. If there were thirty families living in the village in 1911, it was still the largest settlement on The Strip. McOmie in 1914 estimated that 320 people lived in Arizona north of the Colorado River, half of them in Fredonia. Certainly it was the home of many who had participated in the opening of northern Arizona, particularly the Kaibab country. Sharlot Hall did not hesitate to accord the Mormons their "special place in history" for their hard, pioneering labor that had transformed the desert.

Rested, letters written, the wagon repaired, the horses reshod, Sharlot Hall and Al Doyle started out for the Kaibab and the North Rim of the Grand Canyon. They took the direct route by way of Ryan, Nail Canyon, and Big Springs, long used by cattle and sheep men, miners and farmers, and more recently by tourist parties, guided by David D. Rust and E. D. Woolley of Kanab. The route, east of the present highway, is used today primarily as a logging road.

Although the Kaibab Plateau is formed altogether of sedimentary rocks, there are places where low-grade copper deposits have been found. Shortly after 1900, the smelter at Ryan, twenty-four miles from Fredonia, was built to refine ore found near Jacob Lake and other locations, but later the mill was shut down when the metal dropped in price.

Driving up the long, straight, narrow Nail Canyon from Ryan, the travelers camped at Big Springs, one of the largest watering places on the Kaibab. During the day they had passed from the low sagebrush desert, through the zone of piñon and juniper, and here, at nearly seven thousand feet altitude, they were in the lower level of the pine-aspen-spruce forest.

Hall had talked to A. W. Brown, one of the pioneers of Fredonia, and it was probably his son who gave her the Indian lore about the Kaibab. The Arizona Strip was the aboriginal home of the Shoshonean-speaking Southern Paiute Indians. One band, the Kaibab, or Kaibab-its, ranged over the Kaibab Plateau and enjoyed rich harvests of deer and other animals, and wild plant products. Deer were especially plentiful. From the fact that the Indians procured so many hides in the area the Mormon pioneers gave the name Buckskin Mountain to the plateau. John Wesley Powell, who made a systematic study of the tribes during the course of his land surveys, named the plateau after the Indians and that name by now has come into general usage. The Indians themselves referred to the pleateau as "The Mountain Lying Down."

I am not familiar with the great forest fire that Sharlot mentions in the story of the "forester son," Scott Brown. Her one-sentence description of the ride leaves one as breathless as the son must have been when he arrived. Forest fires, somehow, don't seem to get into the histories.

◦§ AUGUST 13. The horses were stiff this morning from the rough trip over the mountains and we found one axle bent and the harness broken— to say nothing of the brake blocks worn off entirely. The load had shaken around in the wagon till the canned goods looked like beaten eggs when I opened the cans. We are evidently immune to tin poison for the heat and jolting has made all our canned stuff taste like a tin shop in full blast, but it is all we have to eat and we have to stand it. The bacon has melted and run out on the wagon box and the crackers are pounded fine enough to roll fried oysters in, and the bread we bake over the sage brush fire tastes like old-fashioned vermifuge, but still we are alive.

About noon we hailed a wagon coming across the valley and found that we were about fifteen miles from Fredonia. Before dusk we came in sight of the tall green Lombardy poplars that mark every Mormon settlement in northern Arizona and presently drove into the greenest, cleanest, quaintest little village of about thirty families.

It seemed too good to be true; the horses thrust their heads into the open ditch and drank till it seemed they could go all the rest of the trip; and I was directed to a trim and comfortable house under the tall trees where a sweet-faced woman welcomed me as cordially as if I had been an old friend. Here in the little hotel I found all the old Western hospitality. It didn't matter that I was caked with red sand and sunburned, and tired from the walking of past days,—I was made comfortable at once and given a better supper than any city hotel could have offered.

AUGUST 14. It seemed so queer to sleep in a bed again that I was ready to get up early and look at the town. It lies in a little valley floored with red sand and walled in by sandstone cliffs banded from red to cream like sash ribbon. The green trees are vivid against the cliffs and the very streets are red sand. However, everything grows in this bright-colored soil and the streets are lined with ditches which distribute the water brought from Kanab Creek through a canal several miles long.

The frame houses are built like cottages in an eastern village and each one has its garden and fruit trees and flowers in bloom. There is a small store with a fair stock of goods and a nice schoolhouse and a church. The whole place has a picturesque charm that is not often found and this most northerly of Arizona towns is also one of the prettiest.

The fields of alfalfa and grain lie outside the town along the bit of level valley and are dotted over with haystacks, showing that crops have been good. Almost every one of the home lots has a big barn at the back full of fresh hay and the whole place looks thrifty.

AUGUST 16. Spent the past two days looking over this valley and letting the horses rest up for a trip of about two hundred miles over the Kaibab Plateau to the northern rim of the Grand Canyon.

I have found many real pioneers here; some of the families were among the settlers on the Muddy River in the early sixties when it was Pah-Ute country. Most of them came into this valley from 1882 to 1885 and settled at Kanab, just across the Utah line seven miles away. Later the good land down here led them to take out a ditch below the one which supplies the Kanab farmers and start this little town.

This whole valley has great possibilities, especially for dry farming and

64

much of the land has been located, though as it is not surveyed no real title can be gotten. The soil is a sandy loam as red as the sandstone cliffs from which it has been eroded but it seems to be very rich. The grass has been trampled out years ago by big flocks of sheep brought in from Utah and by cattle that over-stocked the range, but the summer rains start a good growth of weeds and keep the sage brush growing.

Near Kanab the "spider plant" (*cleome pungens*) [now *c. serrulata* and *c. lutea*], common to all of Arizona, was higher than the high top of our wagon and was growing in sand a foot or two deep. The orchards here all look healthy and thrifty and the fruit is as fine as the best in California or the Salt River Valley.

The settlers here have had the usual trouble to get their irrigating canals built and have had them washed away repeatedly by heavy floods down Kanab Creek. Probably with sufficient capital enough water could be developed to water all the best land of the valley but it is wonderful what these people have done with their own labor.

I am constantly impressed with the courage and persistence of the Mormon colonists; they have good, comfortable houses here that have been built with the hardest labor and in the midst of floods and drouth and all sorts of discouragement. The time will come when new methods of farming and of developing water will cause all the land up here to be used for it is one of the most beautiful valleys I have seen in Arizona and has a fine climate the year 'round; but these first settlers deserve a special place in history for the way in which they have turned the wilderness into good farms and homes.

I expect to spend more time here on my return from the Kaibab, for I am more impressed every day with the value of this part of the "Arizona Strip."

AUGUST 17. Major Powell used the town of Kanab, some seven miles from Fredonia, as a source of supplies when he was exploring the Grand Canyon, and I have found here several people who remember him and quite a number who know the region south to the Grand Canyon very well. What they have told me of the great forest which covers the Kaibab Plateau, and of the copper mines, building stone, agate beds, and also the natural beauty of the whole region has made me decide to see as much of it as possible without too much loss of time.

The beauty of the region has attracted enough attention that each year a few parties of tourists come in from the cities in Utah and make the trip over the mountains and down to the canyon, in spite of the difficult traveling.

Most of them go on horseback, outfitting at Kanab with Woolley and Rust, who have lately built a trail down to the river and operate a cable by which it is possible to cross to the southern bank near the trails coming down from El Tovar.

It is about a hundred miles from Fredonia to the rim of the canyon and there is a wagon road which we shall follow, though it is now in very bad condition from the heavy storms that cut and wash the trails and roads all over the region. Two years ago the road was put in repair and a party came from Salt Lake in automobiles and drove to the canyon by this route, the first machines to reach the northern rim.

The forest ranger has warned us that the grades are in bad shape and we are leaving everything which we can possibly spare here at Fredonia. We have had the wagon overhauled and all the bolts and nuts tightened for the rough road and the ponies freshly shod for the journey and started out with a pleasant young girl as our guest for the day. We are to leave her tonight at Big Springs in Nail Canyon, where her brother is the forest ranger and has his summer camp. Today I have realized more than ever the bigness and wildness of this country; our road led off southwest from Fredonia over a long valley padded with red sand and cut with clay, round hills, dotted with scrub cedars, and long ridges of red sandstone whose erosion has made the bright-colored floor of the country. There is little grass. Like other parts of Arizona this region has been "sheeped to death" years ago and the grass roots trampled out, but there is a great deal of the sage, both black and white, and the new growth of it makes beautiful bands of soft gray-green against the red earth. The stockmen depend on this sage for their winter feed and when it fails both cattle and sheep suffer.

Looking back we could see two bright green spots against the cliffs where the tall Lombardy poplars marked the site of Fredonia and Kanab; north and east the gorgeous cliffs ran for miles, broken now and then with bulky peaks still redder, if that had been possible. For the length of a whole range a strata of cream white stone banded the red like a sash, as if Nature had dressed these cliffs for some fine holiday.

Some day there will be farms over this valley and the little mesas and flats that lie in the finger-like foothills of the Buckskins. Already the dry farming experts from Utah have inspected this region and pronounced it an ideal climate and soil for this sort of agriculture, and much of the land has been temporarily located by young men from the towns along the border.

We stopped for noon near White Sage Flat, where some young men had

66

good crops of corn and potatoes growing, without water for house use ever, and without rain so far this year. Their crops looked well and two of the boys had been so eager to get the land that they rode out from Fredonia to locate one night and called their fields the "Midnight Farms."

From "Midnight Farms" the hills roll and the shallow canyons trend toward the square bulk of the Buckskin range, black in distance with the forest of pines and cedar that cover it down to the lower slopes. Up a long, long shallow canyon and in the shadow of the huge red cliffs that suddenly appeared again, we sighted the abandoned mining camp of Ryan, or Coconino City, where a big smelter and leaching plant was built about ten years ago to work the blanket ledges of copper in the vicinity. The camp has been remarkably well built for a place many miles from a railroad or supplies; it looked like the little military posts scattered over the Apache country of southern Arizona. And no Apache ever had wilder and more beautiful mountains to hide in, nor was better supplied with acorns and piñon nuts.

The water is piped down from Big Springs, six miles up Nail Canyon, and there is a supply ample for the largest mill. The main ledges are some miles back in the hills, but enough ore is piled around the mill to pay, it is said, for the money expended in getting in the machinery. It cannot be worked by the method for which this plant was planned and it has not been regarded as profitable to freight in other machinery over the long mountain road between the mine and the railroad, some 250 miles.

A more beautiful location for a camp could hardly be imagined; it lies on a little bench of foothills ample for mill and town, with a good canyon below for slag dump room. Behind the red cliffs wall the mountain and below rolling hills break away to the sage brush flats, and mountain and hills have enough cedar and piñon for fuel for many years.

The ledges are blanket and low-grade, with here and there a rich bunch and some barren areas—all will probably be worked when transportation is easier.

Beyond Ryan the road wound up Nail Canyon, named for a Mormon family who used to have stock ranches higher up. It is a deep, narrow canyon with limestone cliffs and a scattering of pines growing thicker and taller as we went, till we came to a log fence enclosing a field of alfalfa and oats a mile or two long and a hundred yards wide—like the fields of Arkansas, where the farmer carries his grub and blankets on the plow and runs a furrow down one day and back the next.

The road pushed out against the hill, ran on endlessly till it reached a dim light and the barking of dogs and laughing of children and a group of tents and long cabins, where we left our pleasant girl with her people and made a hasty camp to get up my tent and out-race the rain that hissed and sputtered in the camp fire as I cooked our belated supper.

AUGUST 18. All night between the fall of rain on the tent and the roar of wind in the pines I heard the running of water. This morning it seemed as much overhead as the clouds up the cliff; back of the house ran a carpet of green like a velvet curtain let down from the white lime cliff of the canyon rim and the gurgle and rush of water came down muffled in the dense thicket of stinging nettles tipped with purple blossoms like baby cat-tails, the hop vines clambering over tall wild rose bushes and mingling their pale green clusters of hops with the glossy red rose haws, and the blackberry runners woven in and out like barbed wire.

Perhaps a hundred feet up this green-draped cliff a regular halfgrown river of crystal-clear, icy water bursts out in jets and gurgling streams and leaps down a wooden sluice with such force that when I put my hand in the spray flew up and gave me a second face washing for nothing.

Up in the cliff above the spring are some prehistoric cave dwellings in shallow breaks in the rim, and from the top the trees of Kanab show again though nearly fifty miles away. Wonderful views those old cliff people had over that red, red land of fantastic cliffs and troughlike valleys behind a wild, brilliant land of tameless spirit, as some pagan queen.

I came near sliding from top to bottom of the green wall below the spring; it was hard to look out for my feet when there were pearly snails on every knob of rock and birds new to me were darting out and in among the tangle of vines. I lost my balance once and a grip on the stinging nettles stopped my fall and also reminded me of Kipling's story of the missionary in India who innocently set his converts, who had never worn clothes, to weave themselves garments of a stinging nettle. They ended by jumping in the river—I went to the witch hazel bottle for comfort.

The forester here, Scott Brown, whose father is one of the pioneers of Fredonia and of the old-time West, gave me a record of the settlement of the older places on the Buckskin and told me a good deal about the Pah-Ute Indians, who used to make it their hunting ground. Kaibab, he said, is a Pah-Ute word for deer, and I remember that somewhere Major Powell tells of choosing it because the Indians he met called this the Kai-bab, or "deer" mountain because they got most of their venison and buckskins from it.

I was much impressed in Fredonia with the rarely fine pioneers which I met there; I doubt if any other part of the west has so many of the truest pioneers as Arizona and southern Utah. Mr. Brown's father had followed the frontier from the time of the wars with the "Sacs and Foxes" in Iowa; had walked across the plains to Salt Lake and then explored eastern Nevada and northern Arizona when the Diggers and Pah-Utes and Navajos were ready to make short shift with any white man.

As he told me of his work among the forest summer and winter I was reminded of the story which the gentle little English mother had told me in Fredonia of her forester son. He was one of the forest service men called from his own district to help fight the awful fire which swept the north-western forest last year and cost nearly a hundred lives, beside the vast property loss.

He was out on the Kaibab when the word came, but he rode in to Fredonia as fast as his horse could take him, got food, outfit and fresh horses, said goodbye to wife and children and parents, and was on the road again, riding through the night without sleep or rest, still pushing on by day and night the long distance to the railroad, then still on to the post of duty far in advance of what had been thought the quickest time he could make—and his service there befitted the blood of which he came—the pioneers who tamed the West and left others to tell the story.

EIGHT

Along the North Rim

The great Kaibab Plateau—the "mountain lying down" of the Paiutes—is an elongated upwarp extending all the way across the Arizona Strip from the north rim of the Grand Canyon to the Utah border. It rises from two to four thousand feet above the desert country bordering it and its dark, heavily forested crown running for miles at a height of more than eight thousand feet dominates the skyline as viewed from either side. During the summer months, when the deserts below are baking in the heat, the upper Kaibab is a wonderful, cool island in the sky. It is indeed an "exquisite bit of earth," and no one has described its summer delights better than Sharlot Hall. One of the fairest places is V. T. Park (now De Motte Park, a name given by Powell).

There are few living streams on the Kaibab. Rain and melting snow sink into the plateau's porous limestone surface. But there are a number of small lakes, none as large, however, as Montezuma's Well, a sunken lake in the Verde Valley, and a national monument.

Reaching the Grand Canyon, the travelers spent four days along the forested North Rim enjoying spectacular vistas of the great gorge from prominent viewpoints between Bright Angel Point and Point Imperial. "Uncle Jim" Owens was their guide. After the failure of the cattalo experiment, Jim took a job as warden and hunter in the Grand Canyon Game Preserve established by Congress in 1906. Jim was expected to protect the deer herds and kill off the mountain lions and other predators. He headed a number of cougar-hunting parties on the Kaibab. Among them was one composed of his old friend "Buffalo" Jones and the eastern tenderfoot Zane Grey. Drawn to life in the open, Grey began to write. His first book, The Life of a Plainsman (1908), in which Jim Owens does figure, actually was a biography of Jones.

The South Rim, served since 1901 by a spur from the main line of the Santa Fe Railway, was the goal of most Grand Canyon visitors. Recreational development of the opposite rim lagged. In an attempt to promote North Rim tourism, some enterprising Utahns, David D. Rust and E. D. Woolley among them, built a trail from the rim down through Bright Angel Canyon and then strung a cable across the Colorado, hoping to attract cross-canyon traffic. They opened the route in 1907 but customers were few indeed.

Sharlot Hall and Al Doyle were among the early tourists to the remote North Rim. Sharlot, we note, leaves us with few impressions of the Grand Canyon. She writes of the distant vistas of the San Francisco Peaks and the neighboring volcanic mountains as seen from Greenland Point (now Cape Royal on the Walhalla Plateau). Looking east from Skidoo Point (later renamed Point Imperial) she was so enthralled with the distant view of the Echo Cliffs, the Painted Desert and the great, jagged gorge of the Little Colorado that she "almost forgot" the Grand Canyon dropping away at her feet four thousand feet to the Colorado River.

⋙ FROM BIG SPRINGS our road led up Nail Canyon for fifteen miles, every mile the canyon growing shallower till it seemed only a grassy meadow between gently rolling hills, dimpled and smoothed and almost free of rocks and green and soft as a lawn. The pines and fir trees stood in groups and the white-barked quaking aspen, the "quakenasps" of local speech, wandered out over the grassy level of the bottom or clustered in little swales.

On tiny shoulders of the round hills the little trees stood like school children in thickets so close one could scarcely push through, their limbs all springing from almost exactly the same height and the smooth young trunks white as if newly painted. They had an exquisite youth about them, a sweet and gracious childishness almost human—a picnic group of boys and girls in holiday clothes could not have been more delightful.

Under the big quakenasps the thick, tall grass stood knee deep, with white-flowered yarrow among it and daisies blue as the sky overhead, and asters in many shades from pale blue to purple. The wind ran over them in little puffs and tossed and tumbled them as in play, all so child-like that I could have thought it the spirit of some happy little child—some little Pah-Ute or cliff-dweller whose agate arrow tips I found among the flowers.

I walked all the morning far ahead of the wagon, alone with the moun-

71

tain; when I grew tired I lay down in the grass and rested, and thought that it would be lovely to be buried in such a serene and yet majestic spot, the flowers dancing above and the quakenasp leaves tinkling like little silver bells.

Never have I seen a more exquisite bit of earth than the upper miles of Nail Canyon, park and trees and low-rounded hillsides. The great quakenasps were all scarred by the names of cowboys and with cattle brands of the ranches that used to be here long ago, cut deeply with pocket knives into the bark. It seemed sad, the poor names that mean nothing now—yet each seeking brief record of its owner.

Higher up the silver firs came in, regal as a lovely woman, and once two huge trees sprang from one trunk and one set of intertwined roots—a forest marriage, noble and serene—one might wish them an undivided death as well as life.

Two baby pine squirrels played like kittens up and down a spruce tree, little slate gray fellows with white striped tails. They ran out on the branches and spatted and clawed each other and rolled over and over on the broad spruce branch.

The canyon narrowed presently to a mere tunnel in the green forest, just wide enough for the wagon to pass. Beside ran a little cattle trail and I walked in this; the soft firmness of a forest path trodden by wild things is like no other pavement to the foot, springy and full of life and zest—the feet are glad in going.

When the tunnel was deepest and greenest my guide called softly from his seat in the wagon and just ahead on the hillside stood a deer, a doe, looking at us with curious eyes. She was the reddest deer I have ever seen, red almost as a cow; she had been coming down the road and stopped at sight of us. She seemed full of wonder, especially of me as I walked, then she bounded off like a rubber ball, springing high in the air with big eyes looking and long ears listening for danger.

Some miles on the road wound through Dry Lake Park, where we found many cattle gathered around an almost dry water hole and watered the horses at a "well full of wiggle tails," which the forester had told us we would find in a pen of logs beside an old log cabin. A mile or two beyond we came to the big log corrals of the cattle company and just inside the bars was a young deer licking salt with the cows.

The spruce trees and firs thickened as we came on up a long narrow canyon; the white spruce frosted like fir was wonderfully lovely and graceful, so tall and symmetrical and slender and pointed—so like some dainty lady with many-ruffled skirt all lace edged. The dainty baby trees two and three feet tall and each perfect to the last needle looked like little children in their Sunday clothes, wee babies just learning to walk, and fluttering their little dresses in play as the wind passes.

The flowers are those of the upper zone, much quinine bush, of which the Mexicans and the pioneers use the bark in a tea for fevers, wild roses full of red haws, a sort of yellow aster and purple asters from faint lavender to deep red-purple rich as wine. The daisies in pale blue and lilacs, blue brodiaea, and an exquisite grass flower delicate as a snow crystal.

AUGUST 19. We camped last night in a little glade among the spruce trees and several times I heard a great, wild baying off among the trees—a lobo wolf probably, for they follow the cattle herds and a hunter is kept in this forest reserve just to hunt down them and the mountain lions. I have heard the cry of a mountain lion but this was quite different.

I found some very perfect fossil shells this morning as I walked ahead of the wagon as usual. There are several kinds of spruce trees, or perhaps some of them are fir, and the largest quakenasp trees I ever saw anywhere. Not a bit of timber has been cut in this region except as the forest rangers or cattle camps use a little for cabins and fencing. At noon we came to V. T. Park, where the cattle company has a ranch and the ranger has a comfortable and picturesque log cabin.

The stockmen were out on the fall roundup and we met bands of cattle being driven out for shipment. All this region is forest reserve and only a stated number of stock are allowed on it. It has evidently been greatly over-stocked in the early days when there was no control but the range is improving.

V. T. Park is a narrow, almost level valley running for seven miles between low hills, thickly forested with spruce. Here we came upon the first of the curious "sink hole lakes," which the cattlemen had told us of. They are round or nearly round basins that make one think of the vent of a volcano, except that they occur in the level meadows and have sides as softly curved as artificial pools. They fill with rain and snow water and are very valuable to the stockmen. We passed several today and also some not more than twenty feet across and only two or three feet deep and quite dry—looking exactly like the buffalo wallows of the plains.

They say that in flood season "the bottom falls out" of some of these lakes and the water all runs away underground. We saw one of considerable size that seemed to drain into a crack in the earth at the bottom of the basin, though water marks on the sides indicated that it had once held a good quantity of water. The whole formation of this mountain is limestone and I suppose they are akin to Montezuma's Well and other limestone caverns that fall in at the top and form sink holes or "wells."

Once or twice I have had glimpses of the walls of the Grand Canyon. We are near it now. The spruce trees grow thicker and a new kind with shaggy needles like uncombed sleepy-heads has begun to mingle with the others. The bracken fern is two or three feet tall and touched brown with frost in many places.

The road entered another tunnel-canyon of green trees and cattle, so fat that they shook at every step, ran along before us and stopped to look at the wagon. I had to stop walking because they grew too inquisitive. They all turned aside at a pair of bars and we saw the top of the forester's cabin in front of some tall trees in a little meadow all covered with white yarrow. We drove in and unharnessed and hurried camp because the whole Colorado River seemed coming up in one big rain cloud.

AUGUST 20. It rained last night and while I was hunting pitch wood to start the breakfast fire and my guide was hunting the ponies two pine squirrels came out of a big nest of spruce tips in the tree right over camp and chattered like a pair of weather prophets. The nest was two feet or more across and they sat on the edge and said "Chee-che-chee," in sharp bird-like notes. While they were talking a lot of blue jays seemed to be holding a political meeting in the trees near, and a hawk flew over chased by a pair of humming birds. He lit in a little while in a spruce tree near and they buzzed around like mad bumble bees till he flew and then they followed him across the meadow to a tree on the farther cliffs scolding for all they were worth.

AUGUST 21. We are only a few hundred yards from the great northern rim of the canyon but the forest is so dense that our camp seems in a park on a mountain top. All the water here is in little canyons that cut into the rim in ragged notches.

Our horses scrambled down over a rough trail to a pool of clear water cold as the snow it had melted from and I went on above by a winding rope of path till the whole southern rim seemed to float out of the distance and the purplish blue vapor that filled the lower gorge.

We could see the trail up from the river to El Tovar and the buildings there and at Bright Angel Camp fourteen miles across on an air line but nearly five hundred miles away by the wagon road which we had been obliged to follow. The smoke from a train on the Grand Canyon railroad drifted out and seemed strange enough—"so near and yet so far."

In the afternoon three big hounds came baying into the tent and leaped around in the friendliest way and James T. Owens, the Game Warden of the Kaibab Forest Reserve, rode into camp to guide us over the plateau where a stranger would be lost before he knew it.

He unlocked the door of his log cabin and insisted on getting supper for us while I looked at the border of paws and skulls that bordered the wall near the ceiling. The skins had been stripped off and it was only by the size that I could tell which were mountain lion and which were wildcat and lynx; the skulls too looked grim enough with the dried muscles looking like a mummy face.

Mr. Owens is one of the few genuine trappers and hunters of the old days; "The Last of the Plainsmen" as the novelist, Zane Grey, whom Mr. Owens guided on trips after most of his unique material, called him in a fine story, based on the life of the Game Warden and his many adventures with the wild animals of the plateau.

While we ate supper on a real table he told us that as a boy he trapped and hunted in Texas with an uncle who belonged to the day of Boone and the great hunters of the fur trade; then, still a boy, he lived on the ranch of Charles Goodnight and helped Mrs. Goodnight feed the first stray buffalo calves that followed the cattle to the corrals. Mrs. Goodnight cared for the hungry little waifs out of pure pity at first and no one thought of a herd of tame buffalo; but after a while Mr. Goodnight began to experiment with the crosses on domestic cattle and in these Mr. Owens shared till he is now perhaps as good an authority on the subject as anyone living and owns the buffalo herd which we had found long before in the House Rock Valley beyond Lee's Ferry.

AUGUST 22. Today we started out on the trail to Greenland Point, through a forest where never a tree has felt the axe. The canyon sides were hidden in masses of fir and spruce and yellow pine more thinly covered the level. The plateau is crossed back and forth with sharp canyons that run like a checkerboard in every direction and often seem to end against some cliff without reaching the rim.

Strangers wandering in this maze, with the rim hidden half the time by the forest, can get hopelessly lost in no time. There are few trails that do not just end at some spot where cattle water in summer and the dozens of

75

great limestone cliffs jutting out into the main canyon make it pretty sure that no stranger would ever find the greatest of them alone.

From Greenland Point the southern rim takes on a larger grandeur than one could have imagined, though it is still some two thousand feet lower than the white spur on which we stood when the ride was done. The San Francisco Peaks and the group of peaks to the west and east of them stood up on their plateau as if raised on some vast stage, the highest peaks streaked with snow and cut with blue black lines of canyons that looked like ledges of black rock. We could see all the mountains west to Seligman Peak and perhaps some of the lower chains of hills were even farther west, and seen from the northern plateau they seemed more stern and rugged in outline than from any point in the region south of them.

We had to leave our horses tied to trees back from the rim and walk out to the end of the point, and all along the ground was strewn with fossilized shells and crinoids, and the cliffs were of grayish white limestone overgrown with most beautiful lichens, black, orange, and sage green.

August 23. We rode today to Bright Angel Point where a very fair trail goes down to the river where Messrs. Rust and Woolley have a cable and "skip" by which persons and animals are sometimes taken across the river. So far the trip has not attracted a great number of people but the cable is being improved each year and it is only a matter of time when many visitors to the hotels on the southern rim will cross and spend a few days on the northern plateau and return to leave the canyon by the present railroad.

The roar of Bright Angel Creek comes to the top of the point and there are several falls along the trail down which the water plunges and boils in foamy beauty. From the bottom the vast cliffs rise sheer for a thousand or two feet in one wall and the coloring all along is almost more beautiful than from the better-known southern rim.

August 24. Today we took a pack outfit of two horses with food for several days and started for "Skiddoo Point," which in spite of its name is the most beautiful point along this part of the canyon. The forest too was tall and unbroken except for little natural glades and shallow canyons with grassy bottoms like the ravines of the plains country. In these the bracken fern grew in island-like clumps and asters from palest blue to purple were in full blossom, with many other flowers. The beauty of the whole way was a constant delight.

As we neared the rim the Painted Desert came into view to the east and lying some four or five thousand feet lower than this point which is said to be nine thousand feet above the sea. I almost forgot the vast and gorgeously colored chasm at our feet, the distant view was so strange and bewildering and yet so beautiful.

Echo Cliffs along which we had journeyed from Tuba City to Lee's Ferry and which had towered above us in very good-sized mountains were now in the northern wall of the desert and showed to be the ragged, broken edge of a "fault" where the earth had cracked and sunk and sagged away till it looked like a long piece of broken pie crust,—which may not be a very elegant description but is exactly what it is like, though burned and browned into the richest reds and purples veiled over with a haze even more wonderful that that which hangs always over the canyon.

Rolling westward from the cliffs, the desert dips into rounded hills and shadowed canyons like a bird's-eye view of some gigantic, frozen sea, but a sea of deeper reds and blues and streaked with brighter lines than anything but wet colors on an artist's canvas could show.

No words can tell how weird and unearthly it looks, much as the moon may be, for to the southern edge the round crater cone of Black Butte stands out against the brighter color so distinct that the purple mirage around it seems almost volcanic smoke.

Cutting the gorgeous desert clear across, the canyon of the Little Colorado seems another great break in the earth, ready to fall away perhaps and leave another "fault-line" of peaks and another Painted Desert of rich-colored fragments. But however it seems to waver in the warm, bright haze it never becomes anything but a bottomless pit with jagged walls and dark side-canyons where at a point or two one may see the river in a silver streak.

By moonlight it was still more wonderful and I could scarcely leave the rim to go to bed, and when I did the forest under the moon was so fine I wanted to stay up to watch it.

NINE

Jim Owens: The V. T. Ranch and Jacob Lake

Probably very few readers of this book have ever savored barbequed bob-cat; as cooked by Uncle Jim Owens, Sharlot Hall liked it far better than her first lobster! Owens, whose company Hall and Doyle had shared for several days, was the best-known figure on the Kaibab for nearly twenty years. An early boost to his fame as guide and lion hunter came from Shar-lot's warm portrait of the man. To her the Old Hunter seemed to step right out of the pages of Irving's Astoria.

Sharlot's enthusiasm for the wildlife of the Kaibab Plateau is everywhere evident in these pages. But, along with her contemporaries, she took sides against the lions and other predators—the "varmints." "The good of the lion killing" in the long run meant, however, that the deer, their natural enemies removed, would overstock the range. The threat may be read in Sharlot's words when she says "We saw little fawns in groups like calves." Within ten years government hunters were sent to kill the overpopulation.

Sharlot here gives us some additional details on the buffalo experiment which at the time was viewed with considerable optimism. The herd was first pastured on the higher levels of the Kaibab but the animals did not like the forest and they were moved to the treeless range in House Rock Valley.

The bountiful range of the Kaibab Plateau was first exploited by Mor-mon pioneers who, basing their operations in Fredonia, Kanab and Order-ville, put cattle on the Buckskin as early as 1877. The V. T. Cattle Company, a Mormon outfit, had been ranging herds on the Kaibab for nearly twenty-five years when Sharlot visited their summer headquarters in V. T. (De Motte) Park. E. D. Woolley of Kanab, mentioned frequently, invested in cattle, sheep, and the tourist business.

On their return to Fredonia Sharlot and Al traveled by way of Jacob Lake, one of the more prominent "sink-hole" lakes on the Kaibab, the site of early lumbering, grazing and mining operations. The lake is a mile from the present village of the same name at the junction of highways 67 and 89A. As the travelers left the Kaibab by way of Warm Springs Canyon, Sharlot walked and even "ran on ahead of the team" admiring the rocks and fossils, trees and flowers. A fitting climax to the Kaibab experience came when Sharlot found herself "running down grade like some Atalanta," the swift-footed girl of Greek legend who vowed to marry only the suitor who could outrun her. Rounding a point she discovered that the "full glory" of the country to the north came into view. In the distance, more than twenty miles away, the villages of Fredonia and Kanab were indicated by the tall, green Lombardy poplars. Beyond, pushing the "horizon up into the middle of the sky," three rows of cliffs—Vermilion, White and Pink—marked the headwaters of the Grand Canyon tributaries north of the Colorado River.

৵§ AUGUST 25. We rode today far through the forest to a side-canyon in which our hunter-guide has found many mountain lions and where we hoped the dogs might stir one out. Mr. Owens once climbed out up the rugged walls of this canyon with the fresh skins of three mountain lions on his back and carried his gun and pistol beside.

He found some lion pups in a cave here and was lying flat on his back to twist them out like rabbits with a stick when the dogs scented the mother and she made for the cave in such haste that she didn't see Mr. Owens at all but clawed his back as she went in. He managed to get both her and the pups but it was at closer quarters than was pleasant.

It is here in this forest that Buffalo Jones, who is a life-long acquaintance of Mr. Owens, roped his mountain lions a few years ago and some of them were gotten in this very canyon. We found nothing but a young bobcat which the dogs treed and which Mr. Owens killed and this evening roasted over the camp fire for their supper. They seemed to know just what was going on and watched the sizzling game on the hot coals, pushing close to the fire till it was ready to be cooled and eaten.

I tried to get a picture of the roast cat stuck full length on a green stick over the bed of red pitch chunks. The heat made it turn a little and it looked so like a child being cooked over the fire by cannibals that I thought of David Livingstone and his journeys in the African forests. The flesh and fat were white and delicate as fat lamb and the bobcat feeds only on fresh-killed meat, so when the Old Hunter, as I always called him to myself, cut off a piece for himself and asked me to taste it I didn't mind half as much

79

as the first shrimps I ever ate and not a hundredth part as much as the squirmy red lobster which I was told went into the pan alive. The bobcat was fine, and a young mountain lion is better—as both the Hunter and I knew from past experience.

The trappers of "Astoria" seemed to step out of the shadows as I watched the old man and his dogs; his spare, wiry body pliant as a yew bow and strong as woven sinew; face firm and clean, long and square; big nose with fire and courage in the curve, square chin of fine firmness, mouth as clean of evil lines as the mouth of a fine boy. A face kind as the sun, an outdoor face full of the spirit of forests and mountains—I liked to provoke the smile and the flash and twinkle in the blue eyes.

That was easy—just get the young forester who had joined our party, a fine mountain-bred Mormon boy from Fredonia, to tell some of the old man's lion-hunting adventures. He would sit and blush and presently move off on pretence of getting more firewood. On one trip with Scott Brown (the brave Fredonia boy who made such a record fighting forest fires for the lives of settlers and brother rangers in the great northwestern fire three years ago) they wounded a big lion—these cougars average two hundred pounds apiece according to the Old Hunter—and it leaped far down the nearly perpendicular cliffs and crawled back on a narrow ledge overhung by the cliff so they couldn't get a shot.

They tied two ropes together and then Owens put the loop around his own waist—for brave Scott Brown is a married man and Owens had no one to leave behind if the lion charged too soon. Dangling over the cliff in Brown's hands he went down to the ledge—it was so low he couldn't shoot till he untied the hindering rope and braced into an easier position. The shot rang out and the smoke puffed up to Brown who saw the slack rope in alarm—and the cougar shot out over the cliff and tumbled over and over for thousands of feet and dropped into the canyon-bottom—as a man might have dropped with luck the other way. It took two or three hours stiff climbing to reach the bottom and find the carcass—torn into ribbons too small to hold anything but a bounty.

This Kaibab Plateau was so full of lions and wolves when the Old Hunter came seven years ago that the stockmen had given up trying to raise horses and even lost grown stock as well as colts and calves. Owens had killed a hundred and eighty-four and trapped and roped a dozen or more alive and they were thinning out.

AUGUST 27. We broke camp to move back toward the Warden's cabin;

the good of the lion killing showed today when we saw little fawns in groups like calves among the bracken clumps and does snuffed at us and bounded away on "rubber-tired legs." One big buck stood for his portrait with patience, even pomposity, and then strolled off as if no camera could really do such a creature justice—which was true.

The grouse have been protected by keeping the bobcats and other prowlers down and they went out of the frost-browned bracken on the sunny, open slopes with whizzing of wings.

The rarest and prettiest sight of the whole day was a white-tailed black squirrel who darted away up a tree into a nest of pine needles like a big whisk broom.

AUGUST 28. We made camp near the black squirrel's home tree and my tent was pitched almost under it. At break of day he was down on the ground preening himself like a bird and whisking here and there like a playing kitten, with the plume of cream white, satiny tail arched daintily over his back. They are a little larger than a gray squirrel and the color is really more a beaver-wine than a black. They are so very rare that few naturalists, even, have seen one and the government museums ordered that the Old Hunter should send them a dozen skins for mounted specimens.

He hated mightily to obey that order for he talks to the shy little things as if they were children—but no one else is ever allowed to shoot them, so my morning visitor would wear his sleek fur and vanity plume till some owl or hawk caught him asleep, or age turned him into a white squirrel.

AUGUST 29. We trailed back today to a big spring in a shallow canyon where we shall fix camp and fix up the outfit for the return to Fredonia.

This whole big plateau is a national game preserve and I was interested to know that there have been plans for making it the finest thing of the kind in the world. Likely politics and private jealousy will stop the finest part of the plans but wonderful things might be done.

It is a perfect home for all kinds of game; the whole great forest is checkered through with canyons that give shelter and plenty of water in fine springs; beside the grass and shrubs that deer love the tall bracken fern which is a favorite elk feed grows in all the sunny parks and open spaces.

The Old Hunter reckoned the deer now in the preserve at between seven and eight thousand and none can be shot except when they stray below the reserve line in the short open season in the fall.

He found old elk horns in various parts of the plateau, showing that in the not very distant past elk had lived in the preserve boundaries. For some years Senator [Reed] Smoot, Mr. [E. D.] Woolley of Kanab, Utah, and many citizens of the "Strip" have been trying to get the Government to move elk into this part of Arizona. The isolation of this forest and its whole local condition would make it the finest elk preserve in Arizona.

It was once planned in a tentative way to bring some varieties of African deer and antelope to the plateau from the colder regions of the southern veldt, and Mr. Owens says that his friends who have hunted in Africa believe it might be done with success.

There is no question but a buffalo industry of commercial importance might be worked up if taken at once. The herd in Arizona now is not a government herd as has been rumored, but is a private enterprise.

Some years ago Buffalo Jones, Mr. Owens and a few friends, mostly men who understood the breeding of buffalo with domestic cattle, bought up all the scattered groups in the United States, getting some from the Goodnight ranch, some from Flathead Pablo, an Indian in the Yellowstone region, and some from an old Spaniard in California.

They got from the government a five-year concession to run these buffalo on the Kaibab Forest Reserve and shipped them by way of the Salt Lake road to the station of Lund, where they were uncarred and driven overland to Fredonia and so on into the reserve.

The buffalo thrived and increased, but losses at the hands of outlaws, to whom the value of robes and heads were too great a temptation, caused Jones to remove his part of the herd to a place of his own in New Mexico.

The twenty-six head that remain are owned by Mr. Owens and Mr. Woolley and are ranged chiefly in House Rock Valley, though it is planned to bring them back into the Kaibab another summer.

So far the rapid development of this herd has been hindered by lack of capital for the purchase of the Galloway cows needed. Mr. Owens says he can breed from Galloway to pure buffalo in a short time and could build up a large herd in ten years. This is an enterprise in which the state might well take part; there are range sections of Arizona now producing cattle that could just as well produce buffalo at a thousand dollars a head. Indeed this is too low an estimate of value; a good robe, half or more buffalo, is worth from a thousand to twelve hundred dollars; a good head is worth five hundred dollars, and buffalo meat when it can be had at all is worth forty cents a pound, and a buffalo steer will dress off the range a thousand pounds or more.

There are not half a dozen men living who understand the breeding of buffalo with domestic cattle and a great industry will be lost to the future if some happy chance does not enlist the necessary capital at once. The buffalo and crossbred animals are hardier to cold, short feed, and hardships of all sorts than any domestic cattle, and produce so much more good meat to the animal, that it is a genuine calamity that no real effort is being made to develop them before it is forever too late.

While with the Goodnights in Texas Mr. Owens helped with the breeding of some of the first Persian sheep in the United States and he and Mr. Woolley now have a small herd on the Kaibab from which they expect great things. Like the buffalo, these sheep are larger, hardier, finer meat animals, and bear a valuable skin, making them of much promise as a separate industry, beside the probable value for crossing with some of the mutton breeds now in general use. They are strong, independent-looking fellows and ought to be able to hold their own anywhere.

AUGUST 30. We loaded the wagon and said goodbye to the Old Hunter, with keen regret on both sides for we had too much in common in our memories of the old, forgotten West, not to feel like "kinfolks."

We were going back through "V. T." Park where the V. T. Cattle Company located its headquarters ranch in the early days of the cattle business in the Buckskin country, and where there is now a forest ranger's station as well as the ranch buildings.

The fall rodeo was going on and a lot of stock cattle were being driven out for shipment to other ranges, for the country here, once over-stocked unmercifully in the day of the open range, is being built up to splendid condition by the care of the Forest Service in limiting grazing to what the range will really support.

Some day there will be hundreds of little homes all through these narrow, park-valleys down which our road winds. Just now we are stopped for dinner where the road turns off to the Jacob's Lake sawmill and there are two pretty little places just below us, comfortable log cabins with fields and pasture under "worm fence" or split rails, or pine logs rolled into line. Oats and rye and probably barley would grow anywhere here and as fine potatoes and hardy vegetables as one could wish. The snow is too heavy to stay up all winter but it is only two days' drive down to Fredonia with its good school and pleasant village settlement for winter.

It began to rain as we broke camp after dinner and I walked far ahead of the wagon to gather agates. This stretch of road toward Jacob's Lake has more beautiful agates than any place I have seen in Arizona; they glistened in the rain and I picked up all I could carry and then sorted them out and reluctantly threw away all but the finest. Many of them would cut beautifully and the color and grain are very fine. No doubt they would have some commercial value if gathered carefully.

I found no moss agates but all kinds of banded varieties in an endless combination of colors, some of them the odd "eye" agates that look like an eye, or still more like half a petrified egg with many shadings from yolk to white and a scale of lime for the shell. I found four red stones that very closely resembled raspberries in color and shape and in seed-like wrinkles all over their surface, so natural that I mean to have them set without any cutting on a silver raspberry leaf and have a unique pin of nature's own cutting.

The forest all along has been fine, big yellow pine for the most part. The sawmill at Jacob's Lake is a small one hauled in by wagon years ago, coming probably from Salt Lake. Most of the lumber for Fredonia has been cut here but the mill burned a few weeks ago and new machinery has not yet been put in.

Jacob's Lake is one of the natural pocket lakes helped out by a small artificial reservoir, and it is an old cattle ranch as well as sawmill. From the lake out two or three miles on the road down Warm Spring Canyon we traveled through some of the finest yellow pine seen on the mountain and passed many stringers of a light- sponge-like copper ore in the most vivid greens and blues and yellows. Small cuts have been run along many of these leads but they are thin little blanket ledges and so far nothing worth working has been developed.

The road through Warm Spring Canyon is longer than the one we came up from Fredonia on but it is worth the extra time. For a few miles the canyon was only a grassy trough among the pines where the wind running before a big rain cloud made the tall grass ripple like flowing water; then deepening walls of limestone spotted with black moss and lichens and overgrown with wild vines and shrubs shut us in.

The mountain pines gave way to blue-berried cedar and juniper and scattering groups of true red cedar very graceful and sweet, and to blankets of dark, gnarled piñon pines over every rugged slope.

Though the road plunged over ledges of worn lime rock like waterfalls and kept the boulder-filled bed of the canyon at a swift descent, I ran on ahead of the team, the wind singing down over the trees like some great tide coming in. Asters in all shades of blue, and lavender and yellow *cleome pungens* [lavender = *c. serrulata;* yellow = *c. lutea*] stood tall as my head, and bright penstemons gleamed crimson up in the rocks. Now and again I found fossil shells in the road, worn smooth with passing wheels, for all this lime country is full of small fossils in several varieties.

Running down grade like some Atalanta to whom shells and flowers were only a moment's stay, I wheeled round a point of red hill and the full glory of the country toward Kanab and Fredonia lay unrolled.

No wonder the early Mormon explorers believed that God had revealed to them a land to be all their own—such a land as no white man had called his home—and in which they should build up an empire unlike any upon earth! The red valley dipped and rolled away to the northeast in waves of hill and low canyon streaked with purple gray sage and round-topped cedars—till the mighty sandstone cliffs banded and striped red and brown and cream like a Roman ribbon pushed the horizon up into the middle of the sky. Snow-covered mountains of Utah hung on the haze, and in a gouge in nearer red walls the slender lombardy of Kanab backed the green of alfalfa fields.

The sun was shining over the valley though there was a storm over the mountains behind us and presently we drove out into regular puddles where the rain had just passed, and after driving ten miles in search of a dry camping ground had to pull up under a cedar and make camp in the mud, coaxing a fire with pitch kindling brought down from the mountain.

AUGUST 31. I left our muddy, uncomfortable camp about sunrise while the wagon was being packed and was soon far out on the sage-covered flats toward Fredonia. This lower country is one succession of low valleys and rolling hills and is still a good stock range, though it has been "sheeped to death" since the early eighties and now has scattering bunches of cattle on it. It will someday be a fine belt of dry-land farms; almost in sight of our muddy camp the "dry lander" boys from Fredonia have fine corn and potatoes growing on the newly cleared sagebrush land of Midnight Flats.

TEN

The Kaibab Plateau and Arizona

Here Sharlot Hall ventures to tell the world what the great Kaibab Plateau is worth. Its vast resources are there, waiting for Arizona to develop them. She was careful to point out that the Mormons from southern Utah, headed by such men as Jacob Hamblin, had had a foothold on The Strip before Arizona was made a territory. Perhaps, she predicted, Arizona after so many years of neglect may discover the "wild grandeur and beauty" of the Kaibab by means of that "wonder worker, the automobile."

Roads were the key. Having walked many sandy and rocky miles and bumped along in a wagon over Strip roads, Sharlot pointed out the best routes. By the time she wrote this chapter the government bridge had been put across the Little Colorado below Tanner's Crossing and the way was open for automobiles to reach The Strip by Lee's Ferry. In time the roads were developed and improved and paved. Over every one of the routes on The Strip now paved Sharlot Hall and Al Doyle drove their wagon in 1911.

The patterns of economic development on the Kaibab and the rest of The Strip were pretty clearly cut when Sharlot wrote but her articles did advertise the potentials. Still it required few people to operate ranches, lumber mills and mines and population increases were very slow and the area has remained under the jurisdiction of the two counties, Mohave and Coconino. According to the 1950 census, the population of Arizona's southeasternmost Cochise County was 31,488, an estimated ten times that of the Arizona Strip.

We may conclude safely that Sharlot Hall's description of the great Kaibab started a flow of tourists. Coming in "wonder workers" their numbers increased annually. Few visitors know, probably, that one of the first tourists, and the first to popularize the scenic beauties of the Kaibab, was Sharlot Hall.

~§ I WANT TO INTERRUPT this narrative to speak of the value of this great Kaibab Plateau to the rest of Arizona. Cut off by the huge walls of the Grand Canyon it has remained an unknown land and I question if today a dozen Arizonans south of the canyon have any idea of its character or value.

Geographically it is part of the great tangle of plateaus and valleys, cliff-walled canyons and vast and fantastically eroded mountain ranges which include southeastern Utah and make up a wonderland unsurpassed upon earth, though still almost unknown except to a handful of people.

The Grand Canyon on the south, a scantily-watered region on the west, and one of the wildest canyon-cut deserts known on the east, has made the natural point of entrance from the north and most of the settlers have come from the towns and cattle ranges of southern Utah.

In the early fifties the Mormon Church sent such intrepid men as Jacob Hamblin and his comrades to explore and report upon the region and in the sixties Mormon colonists were called to the Virgin River on the southern border of Utah and made permanent settlements there. Some bands of stock were before long pushed over the line and the struggle began with the Navajo Indians as to whether Indian or white should hold the country.

The Pah-Utes of the Kaibab forest added their portion to the struggle from time to time and the Mormon Church gave aid in building a fort of red sandstone at Pipe Spring, about two miles from the most northerly settlement in Arizona. Having given this region its first and almost its only settlements, having made the only thorough explorations not prosecuted by the U.S. Geographical [Geological] Survey, and having kept watch of the growing colonies through all the years up to the present, the Utah settlers thought it very natural that they should have tried to annex the "Strip."

As a matter of fact Mormon explorers knew this region very well before Arizona was organized as a territory and thrifty settlements were growing cotton in sight of the northern line of Arizona when the pine logs were being cut for the old "Governor's House" at Prescott.

After the half century of neglect it is likely that Arizona will discover her northern wonderland through the medium of that wonder worker, the automobile; and that the varied commercial development which is possible there will follow the pleasure seeker instead of the soldier and explorer of old days.

The great, uplifted plateau of the Kaibab will some day be as great a summer playground as the Yellowstone or the Yosemite; there are dozens

87

of deep side-canyons and projecting points sweeping out over the main Grand Canyon that have not been explored at all and which offer genuine adventure, with the chance of "finds" of mineral, and objects of scientific value. There are good-sized prehistoric cliff-dwellings that have not been entered by a white man; rare cone-bearing trees and great numbers of shrubs and plants that have not been studied and a great variety of material for the geologist and the practical miner.

For the sportsman there is the chance of roping a mountain lion and bringing him out alive on a pack-horse, or of hunting deer with a camera on the largest national game preserve in the world, and one which our Arizona hunters should know and should aid in having stocked with the great variety of game to which it is so admirably adapted.

The wild grandeur and beauty of the region is beyond description; virgin forest, bank upon bank of spruce and fir on mountainside and canyon wall, towering yellow pine over the more level plateau, quaking aspen that are giants of their race in the shallow canyons,—and narrow, grassy flower-sown parks that run like natural roadways back and forth over the whole region.

The whole northern wall of the Grand Canyon (which is the southern boundary of the Kaibab) is from a thousand to three thousand [actually not more than about twelve hundred] feet higher than the southern side and from any point the view southward over the Painted Desert, including the San Francisco Peaks and all the mountains westward, is awe-inspiring in its vast and varied sweep, its gorgeous colors veiled in the ever-changing blue haze, the almost bottomless gorge between making it seem like a view across some stranger planet.

For the present the quickest and easiest way to reach the Kaibab is from the end of the Grand Canyon railroad, going down the trail to the river at El Tovar; crossing the cable to the northern bank, which is only [also?] an interesting experience, and climbing up the Bright Angel trail on the northern side to the camp on the rim where guides and outfit can be had for trips through the forest and for lion hunting excursions. Messrs. Rust and Woolley of Kaibab have built the trail, operate the cable and provide horses and camp outfit, and the game warden of the forest directs the lion hunting.

It is an interesting fact that so far more foreigners than Americans have made this trip and the lions have been sent out alive to parks in England and Germany.

At the present time automobiles have only reached the northern rim by way of wagon road from southern Utah but it is possible at no prohibitive expense to extend the great highways of northern Arizona to make all this wonderland open to auto travel from the south. From Flagstaff privately owned machines now make frequent trips to Tuba City, some ninety miles northward on the wagon road used by the Mormon colonists to Arizona in the seventies, "The Old Mormon Road" as it is still often called.

The Little Colorado River has now a good bridge built by the Government and this end of the road cuts the most beautiful part of the Painted Desert, passing some little-known petrified forests, and remarkable agate beds. From Tuba to Lee's Ferry machines have been taken and the road might be made very fair, following the wild and rich-colored Echo Cliffs to a point below the present ferry where a bridge site has been reported favorable by engineers, or making crossing on the very good ferry maintained by Coconino County.

From Lee's Ferry, which is one of the most beautiful points along the river in richness of coloring, the road winds through a region of remarkable rock erosions, skirts a long mesa where the white walls of Marble Canyon mark the westward course of the river, then follows House Rock Valley over the upper end of the Buckskin Mountains to Fredonia, then southward again to Greenland Point on the northern rim.

There is a road from the Rock House [House Rock] cattle ranch across to Jacob's Lake and so to the Rim which would probably develop into the logical and shorter route. Returning it would be possible to go out to Fredonia, thence to St. George, down past the Grand Gulch mine to the river again at Gregg's Ferry, thence to Kingman—and so have in one trip a great loop over the width of the "Arizona Strip." I have made it by wagon and in California I have seen permanent automobile roads developed over country no more difficult.

There is but one small sawmill in the Kaibab forest at present and over three billion feet of marketable lumber could be cut, according to the Forest Service estimate. For the present it waits the railroad which will probably come from some point on the Salt Lake line, a branch having been recently completed to St. Thomas and surveyed on to St. George. This will lose to Arizona all the business that might be developed by even a first class wagon road leading out to Lee's Ferry.

The whole Kaibab region has been grazed by sheep and cattle since the early eighties and will continue its range value indefinitely, especially since reserve restrictions prevent over-stocking. Probably, much new grazing area might be developed, especially to the westward, by development of water in the regions now remote from springs and where wells have not been attempted.

The agricultural possibilities of the whole great valley lying north of and along the base of the plateau will some day write as fine a chapter in Arizona history as the deserts of the south are writing today.

So far the taxes paid by this "Strip" in the part belonging to Mohave County have been much larger than any expense of government to the county; in Coconino County there has been complaint both from and against the "Strip"—and in both counties the very great distance of the settlements from the county seat and county officers has given rise to inevitable difficulties

The wise and logical solution is to make this entire corner of the state a separate county as soon as possible; with the survey of state lands and means of obtaining titles many settlers will come in, especially from the border of Utah where men are now waiting with their lands all chosen for location as soon as that shall be possible. This region, which was once partly included in Arizona's lost county of Pah-Ute will in its own good future balance up very favorably with its great diagonally opposing county of Cochise—though the latter have half a century the start in the race.

ELEVEN

The Arizona Strip West

After their extended trip to the Kaibab Plateau Sharlot Hall and Al Doyle returned once more to Fredonia. They had been on the road thirty-eight days but had seen less than half of the Arizona Strip. Heading west they visited the Mormon villages and towns scattered along the Arizona-Utah boundary west of Fredonia and Kanab. On September 1, 1911, they camped at Pipe Spring. The big, cut-stone fort built around a spring, one of the best watering places in the area, was a reminder of the Mormon-Indian hostilities of the 1860's and 1870's. It was used primarily as the headquarters of a succession of cattle companies who ranged their herds over The Strip. Sharlot took note that southward from Pipe, "a great valley sweeps away, running on the west to Mt. Trumbull, one of the unknown but truly great peaks of Arizona." The valley, she predicted, would some day provide homes for "hundreds of people, being an ideal farming location."

The travelers visited Moccasin, just north of Pipe Spring and the adjacent Indian school on the Kaibab Indian reservation just recently established. Going on through Cane Beds and Big Plain Sharlot Hall and Al Doyle reached the crest of the Hurricane Cliffs in Utah where they enjoyed magnificent views of the country toward the west. At the base of the cliffs "straight down some fifteen hundred feet, a flat, narrow valley lay below, checkered with green alfalfa fields and orchards and dotted with little white frame and red brick houses."

The green fields around the Mormon village of Hurricane, and La Verkin nearby, where irrigated with waters conveyed through long canals from the Virgin River. Sharlot continued her description of the view from the cliff tops: "I doubt if my eyes will ever look upon a more beautiful scene—it was like looking down on some village in the volcanic region of Italy or Sicily. The huge cliffs were dark with lava flows; crater cones stood up through the red sandstone on the farther side of the valley: great wind-blown banks of bright rose red sand were drifted up the slope of the mountains" to the southwest and walling the valley on the northwest was a "noble mountain range covered to the top with a dark pine forest that looked blue in the distance." Many have admired this view of the valley of the Virgin River and Pine Valley Mountain, though few have described it as well.

Now, with "the vivid red and cream sandstone walls of the Pink Cliffs" hanging "like a painted theater curtain" off to the north, they traveled up the Virgin River to see Zion Canyon. En route they passed through the Mormon villages of Virgin, Grafton, Rockville and Springdale; Hall admired "the massive stone houses" as "quaint as the villages of the old world," and the old trees almost overlapping above the wide streets "so that we drove down tunnels of green shadow." Sharlot recorded few details of her visit to Zion, which had been proclaimed a national monument in 1909 (it became a national park ten years later), but she did mention Cable Mountain where by means of an ingeniously rigged cable, lumber was lowered over two thousand feet from the canyon cliff to the valley floor.

Pressing on through Toquerville and Leeds the travelers "dragged through miles of deep red sand" to St. George, the capital of Utah's "Dixie," where they spent six days. St. George was celebrating the fiftieth anniversary of its settlement and "from all directions covered wagons were coming in with people who had been there fifty years before, or whose parents had —and the village was thronged with a thousand or more strangers." Sharlot Hall found the Mormon Temple at St. George "curiously like the Mission San Xavier [del Bac, near Tucson], and it was built under conditions no less severe and wild and by a people no less zealous." Lumber for its construction came from Mt. Trumbull, "nearly a hundred miles south in Arizona," and was "hauled out over roads that would tire an eagle to fly over." The temple, she wrote, "was one of the most impressive monuments in the Southwest."

Sharlot met a number of influential citizens and learned much about the Mormon pioneers who had first settled the middle reaches of the Virgin River in the 1850's and who, from this base, had extended their frontier eastward across the Arizona Strip eventually reaching the Little Colorado country by way of Lee's Ferry. From here, too, they had opened a corridor to the Pacific by way of Las Vegas. And, more to Sharlot's interest, the Mormons had opened mines along the Grand Wash Cliffs on The Strip well over eighty miles south of St. George.

Hall wanted to see those mines, and on September 14 with Al Doyle, she headed south over some of the roughest country yet visited. It was a tough two-day climb up Moqueak Mountain to Wolf Hole and then it was a lonely two days more—"for a hundred miles we saw no one"—to the Grand Gulch Mine, the main diggings in the area, a copper prospect opened in the 1870's. Like those near Ryan, the ores of the Grand Gulch and neighboring mines were found in sedimentary rock. Sharlot went down into the mine to the two-hundred-foot level and took notes on the smelting and refining operations.

Edging into Nevada, they stopped next at Gold Butte, another mining district which had passed its prime in 1911. At Gregg's (previously Scanlon's) Ferry the travelers crossed the Colorado and once again entered Arizona. Sharlot Hall described the ferry and the crossing: it was a "rickety pile of rotten boards held together with iron bars and poled along the muddy current by two cottonwood poles with bits of slabs nailed on for oar-blades. It was all so exciting that I was not afraid." Heading south up Hualapai Wash they crossed Gold Basin, passed through a dense yucca forest to Dolan Springs, and finally reached Chloride, a bustling silver mining camp in the Cerbat Mountains.

During the next two weeks Sharlot Hall spent busy days in and about Chloride and Kingman, on the mainline of the Santa Fe. She talked to many people, took notes, made photographs, packed and shipped to Prescott specimens gathered along the way, visited Mineral Park, the oldest mining camp in the Cerbats, and the turquoise mines nearby. By automobile she went to visit the mines near Union Pass in the Black Mountains. From a point beyond the pass she enjoyed a commanding view of the valley of the Colorado. Directly below was historic Fort Mohave and Hardyville and south in the distance were The Needles. Across the river parts of both California and Nevada were visible for miles.

Sharlot steeped herself in history and lore. She visited graves of men killed in the Indian wars, she learned of James White's voyage through the Grand Canyon in 1867, and she spent a day and a half digging in the records in the county court house. One afternoon she met with the ladies of Kingman to recount her adventures covering the past two and a half months. Al Doyle in the wagon left for Flagstaff on October 4; Sharlot Hall returned by train to Prescott and Phoenix sometime after October 11, 1911.

Bibliography

Bingham, Edwin R. *Charles F. Lummis, Editor of the Southwest*. San Marino, California: Huntington Library, 1955.

Crampton, C. Gregory. *Land of Living Rock. The Grand Canyon and the High Plateaus: Arizona, Utah, Nevada*. New York: Alfred A. Knopf, 1972.

Dellenbaugh, Frederick S. *A Canyon Voyage: The Narrative of the Second Powell Expedition down the Green-Colorado River from Wyoming, and the Explorations on Land in the Years 1871 and 1872*. New York and London: G. P. Putnam's Sons, 1908.

————. *The Romance of the Colorado River*. New York and London: G. P. Putnam's Sons, 1904.

Easton, Robert, and Brown, Mackenzie. *Lord of Beasts, the Saga of Buffalo Jones*. Tucson: University of Arizona Press, 1961.

Fergusson, Erna. *Our Southwest*. New York and London: Alfred A. Knopf, 1940.

Gordon, Dudley. *Charles F. Lummis: Crusader in Corduroy*. Los Angeles: Cultural Assets Press, 1972.

Grey, Zane. *The Last of the Plainsmen*. New York: Outing Publishing Company, 1908.

Hall, Sharlot M. "Arizona," *Out West*. XXIV (February 1906): 71–135.

————. *Cactus and Pine: Songs of the Southwest*. Boston: Sherman, French, and Company, 1911. Second Edition, Revised and Enlarged. Phoenix: *Arizona Republican*, 1924.

————. "The Camels in Arizona," *Land of Sunshine*. 8 (February 1898): 122–23.

————. *Diary* in "Line a Day" Book. MS, 1908, 1911, and a few later dates: Sharlot Hall Museum, Prescott, Arizona.

—————. "Miss Sharlot Hall Tells Women's Federation of Trip Among Indians . . ." Newspaper clipping dated January 29, 1912.

—————. Box 8 Sharlot Hall MS: Sharlot Hall Museum, Prescott, Arizona.

—————. *Poems of a Ranch Woman Posthumously Compiled* by Josephine Mackenzie. Prescott, Arizona: Sharlot Hall Historical Society, 1953.

—————. *Report of Arizona Historian* to Richard E. Sloan, Governor of Arizona. Report covers period October 1, 1909 to December 31, 1911. Phoenix? n. p., 1912?

—————. *The Story of the Smoki People.* Prescott, Arizona: *Prescott Courier,* 1922.

—————. "Women Who Write of the Early West," *Arizona, the New State Magazine. II* (April 1912): pp. ?

Henson, Pauline. *Founding a Wilderness Capital: Prescott, A. T. 1864.* Flagstaff, Arizona: Northland Press, 1965.

Larson, Andrew Karl. *I Was Called to Dixie. The Virgin River Basin: Unique Experiences in Mormon Pioneering.* Salt Lake City: Deseret News Press, 1961.

Lockwood, Frank C. "She Writes of the Old West," *Desert Magazine.* 3 (December 1939): 3–5, 36.

Loraine, Mrs. M. W. "Arizona's Best Loved Woman," *West Coast Magazine.* IX (January 1911): 293–97.

Lummis, Charles F. "In Western Letters," *Land of Sunshine.* 14 (April 1901): 300–305.

Mackenzie, Josephine, compiler. *Poems of a Ranch Woman by Sharlot Hall with a Biography by Charles Franklin Parker.* Prescott, Arizona: Sharlot Hall Historical Society, 1953.

McClintock, James H. *Arizona: Prehistoric-aboriginal, pioneer-modern. The Nation's Youngest Commonwealth within a Land of Ancient Culture.* 3 vols. Chicago: S. J. Clarke Publishing Company, 1916.

McOmie, A. M.; Jacobs, C. C.; and Bartlett, O. C. *The Arizona Strip: Report of a Reconnaissance of the Country North of the Grand Canyon.* Phoenix: Board of Control, 1915.

Merritt, Evelyn B. *Arizona's First Capitol Preserved by Sharlot M. Hall.* Prescott, Arizona: Prescott Printing Company, 1971.

Parker, Charles Franklin. "Out of the West of Long Ago," *Arizona Highways.* 14 (January 1943): 7–11, 35. Reprinted in Josephine Mackenzie, compilation, *Poems of a Ranch Woman.* (1953).

Peterson, Charles S. *Take Up Your Mission: Mormon Colonizing Along* the *Little Colorado River, 1870–1900*. Tucson: University of Arizona Press, 1973.

Weston, James J. "Sharlot Hall: Arizona's Pioneer Lady of Literature," *Journal of the West*. IV (October 1965): 539–52.

Yavapai Magazine. "An Interesting Interview with Sharlot M. Hall . . .", XII (October 1924): 15–16.

SHARLOT HALL ON THE ARIZONA STRIP
WAS SET IN TEN POINT CALEDONIA
AND PRINTED ON MOUNTIE WARM WHITE TEXT
BOUND AT ROSWELL BOOKBINDING IN PHOENIX